DEDICATION

To God the Father, The Son, and the Holy Spirit
for enabling my FRESH START

FASTTRACK
YOUR
FRESH START
WITH
PRAYER

A 21-DAY PRAYER JOURNEY

DAMOLA TREASURE OKENLA

HILLTOP
Creative Publishers
PUSHING OUT THE MESSAGE FROM WITHIN

HILLTOP
Creative Publishers
PUSHING OUT THE MESSAGE FROM WITHIN

www.damolatreasureokenla.com

Okenla, Damola Treasure, 1966 –

Fast-Tracking Your Fresh Start: 21-Day Prayer Journey

Dominique Lambright: Editor

Dawn James (Publish and Promote): Book Production

Kingdom Branding: Book Cover Design & Interior Layout

ISBN (Paperback) 978-1-948971-06-5

ISBN (eBook) 978-1-948971-07-2

Note to the reader: This book is not intended to dispense psychological or therapeutic advice. The information is provided for educational and inspirational purposes only. In the event, you use any of the information in this book for yourself, which is your constitutional right, the author and publisher assumes no responsibility for your actions. In some chapters, names and locations have been changed to protect privacy.

Printed and bound in the United States

CONTENTS

INTRODUCTION

❋

WHAT IS FRESH START?

Fresh Start could mean "New Dawn", which in the physical realm signifies the new beginning; the appearance of a new day, new month, or new year. In the spiritual, it is the season after an unpleasant experience, that is, the night season of life. For this reason, the Psalmist declared, "Weeping may endure for a night, but joy comes in the morning." It is the beginning of something new.

It is a fresh development.

Fresh is when the light is separated from darkness and morning breaks forth.

"And God said, let there be light; and there was light. And God saw that the light was good (suitable, pleasant) and He approved it; and God separated the light from the darkness." II Corinthians 4:6

"And God called the light Day, and the darkness He called Night. And there was evening and there was morning, one day." Genesis 1:3

"The nights of crying your eyes out give way to days of laughter." Psalm 30:5 MSG

God said, "I command lights to appear in the sky and to separate day from night and to show the time for seasons, special days, and years." Genesis 1:14 CEVDCUS06

The night shall pass, and your morning shall come in the mighty name of Jesus.

IT IS A SEASON OF RE-ALIGNMENT WITH DESTINY or PURPOSE!

IT IS A SEASON FOR RESTRUCTURING!

WHO NEEDS A FRESH START?

Fresh Start is for anyone who refuses to accept life or a situation as it was or is and is ready to strive for the best that life has to offer. Even if it is not visible to them but they are conscious of it and ready to pursue it. In my mind, this is personified by a woman called Ruth.

Fresh Start is for that person who has a larger vision for himself/herself and who is ready to pursue it. This desire reminds me of a man named Jabez.

Fresh Start is for someone who has developed an unstoppable mindset to achieve his/her goals and is ready to push through any obstacles: human, physical, or spiritual. It is for that person who desires self-enhancement, like Jabez did.

Fresh Start is for the individual who wants to activate his/her potential or take his/her potential to a new height like the dead and buried giants in the book of Ezekiel 37.

Fresh Start is for people who are ready to push beyond their current challenges or successes because there is always something to be done, to be discovered, to be pursued and captured, like Blind Bartimaeus in Mark 10:46-52.

Fresh Start is for those who despite their setbacks in life, are determined to achieve their full potential. They have a dream, and they may have lost sight of it, but then they had another dream and kept their hope alive, as Joseph did.

WHEN DO YOU NEED A FRESH START?

• When you feel uncomfortable being in any certain situation that is contrary to your expectation.

• When you find yourself in a position or location without any appreciable progress; even God recognized that the Hebrews were stagnant at a point in their journey to the promised land, and He sent Moses to tell them to move forward.

"The Lord our God spoke to us at Horeb, saying, 'You have stayed long enough on this mountain.'" Deuteronomy 1:6

• When you have made bad decisions or choices that are not helping you.

• When you have gone through distressing situations; it could be in your finances, career, business, marriage, ministry, relationship, or health.

"Arise [from spiritual depression to a new life], shine [be radiant with the glory and brilliance of the Lord]; for your light has come, And the glory and brilliance of the Lord has risen upon you." Isaiah 60:1

• When you know without any doubt that you must be completely honest about your behavioural patterns, but you cannot achieve change by yourself. That was the story of a man called Jacob, a fraudster, swindler, cheated who sought God for a

FRESH START, a new life of a new habit; his story of repentance and demand for a change is found in the book of Genesis in chapter 32.

• When you have gone through seasons of disappointment: Fresh Start is for anyone who wants to rebrand themselves or what they do. Fresh Start is for recovery from loss or any adverse situation, like those faced by both widows in 1 Kings 17:8-16 and 2 Kings 4:1-8. Fresh Start is turning your adversity into an opportunity to change the world around you.

SYMPTOMS OF THE NEED FOR A FRESH START

The presence of some of the situations below could be an indication that you need a FRESH START:

Emotional: depression, anxiety, fear, worry, stress, pressure, anger, grief, low self-esteem, inferiority complex, self-rejection, sense of failure, anxiety.

Physical: body pains, sickness, joint pains.

Cognitive: memory problems, indecision, poor choices, nightmares, lack of concentration, negative thoughts.

Behavioral: eating disorders, withdrawal, new or increased addictions, insomnia, lack of interest.

Fresh Start doesn't just happen. It evolves over time. There are due processes to follow on this journey.

For Ruth, as it was mentioned earlier on, the journey started when she decided to follow her mother-in-law to Bethlehem, so her Fresh Start began with a decision.

DECISION, DECISION, DECISION!!!

Fresh Start is an opportunity to look in a different direction for a better outcome for your finances, career, business, marriage, relationships, family, habits, health, and faith.

It is a time to restart; rekindle, restore, revive. It is a time for newness and freshness.

Someone recently told me that before you can start afresh you will need to answer these questions:

> What happened?
> Why did it happen?
> How did it happen?
> What could have been done better?
> What next?

Another step is to identify the specific area or areas in your life that need change. The question, "How?" is very crucial to your Fresh Start. How do I move on?

> After losing a job?
> After losing a vital relationship?
> After losing a significant person?
> After failing an exam or any adventure?
> After a success?
> After missing an opportunity?

From careful observation and study, I have discovered that Fresh Start is a gradual process and not an instant one, accompanied by:

Discovery (Self-Audit)
Desire
Determination
Devotion
Direction
Diligence
Discipline
Destination (Recovery)

You will also need to answer some other important questions:

Where am I right now?
What can I do better?
What do I know to help facilitate change?
What will I need to do to get it done?
What will be the result of my actions or inaction?
What will be the outcome for me?

Part of what you need to do is to identify people who have achieved things that you desire to achieve, find out what worked for them, and use that information to guide your course of action. That is why we are following the fellows who used the weapon of prayer to secure their Fresh Start.

WHY PRAYER?

To what areas of life can you wield the weapon of prayer?

> Mental
> Emotional
> Financial
> Business
> Marital
> Generational
> Spiritual
> Ministerial
> Academics

The power of prayer can be witnessed through precedent, principle and promise.

Precedent: There are numerous examples in the Bible of people who used prayer as part of their effort to secure their Fresh Start. People like biblical Hannah, who had fertility issues, but prayed and things turned around for her. Today, we have many testimonies from people who prayed and as a result changed their adverse situations. God is still in the business of turning the story to glory, shame to honor, and granting people a Fresh Start if only they will call on Him. Hannah's story is found in the book of 1 Samuel chapters 1-2.

Principle: For a Christian, one of the key principles of the kingdom, as given to us by Jesus, is the weapon of prayer.

"Keep on asking and it will be given you; keep on seeking and you will find; keep on knocking [reverently] and [the door] will be opened to you." (Matthew 7:7)

"Also, when you pray." (Matthew 6:5) Note, not "if" you pray.

And we were told in Luke 18, "Men always ought to pray and not lose heart."

Do not fret *or* have any anxiety about anything, but in every circumstance *and* in everything, by prayer and petition (definite requests), with thanksgiving, continue to make your wants known to God. (Philippians 4:6)

Other supportive scriptures can be found in: John 15:7; 1 Thessalonians 5:16; Jeremiah 29:10 -14)

Promise: Apart from the call to prayer there are promises of answered prayer.

"And it shall be that before they call I will answer; and while they are yet speaking I will hear." (Isaiah 65:24).

"Call to Me and I will answer you and show you great and mighty things, fenced in and hidden, which you do not know (do not distinguish and recognize, have knowledge of and understand)." Jeremiah 33:3

Affliction, adversity, setback, misfortune is not meant to last forever, but they all have a termination date. Prayer terminates their existence because prayer is partnering with God to end such, not just in our lives, but in our environment in the lives of other people.

"And after you have suffered a little while, the God of all grace [Who imparts all blessing and favor], Who has called you to His [own] eternal glory in Christ Jesus, will Himself complete and make you what you ought to be, establish and ground you securely, and strengthen, and settle you." 1 Peter 5:10

"And it shall come to pass That whoever calls on the name of the Lord Shall be saved. For in Mount Zion and in Jerusalem there shall be deliverance, as the Lord has said, among the remnant whom the Lord calls." Joel 2:32

Whoever calls, 'Help, God!' gets help. On Mount Zion and in Jerusalem there will be a great rescue— just as God said. Included in the survivors are those that God calls. (Joel 2:28

He will wipe every tear from their eyes, and there will be no more death or sorrow or crying or pain. All these things are gone forever. And the one sitting on the throne said, "Look, I am making everything new!" And then he said to me, "Write this down, for what I tell you is trustworthy and true." And he also said, *"It is finished! I am the Alpha and the Omega— the Beginning and the End. To all who are thirsty I will give freely from the springs of the water of life. All who are victorious will inherit all these blessings, and I will be their God, and they will be my children."* Revelation 21:4

What a God we have! And how fortunate we are to have him, this Father of our Master Jesus! Because Jesus was raised from the dead, we've been given a brand-new life and have everything to live for, including a future in heaven—and the future starts now! God is keeping careful watch over us and the future. The Day is coming when you'll have it all—your life will be healed and whole.

In every situation there is always an opportunity to advance, but you must carefully observe and embrace that opportunity. A man who has been blind for most of his life cannot afford to miss the opportunity of regaining that sight when he realizes that Jesus is passing by and this could be his last chance. (Mark 10:46-52)

I don't know about you, but I need a Fresh Start in this season of my life. I have had many Fresh Starts in my life, having gone through a series of life-changing experiences, bad relationships, failed expectations, and mistakes. I cannot afford to stay any longer in the rut.

I remember when I was in a particularly bad relationship that I should not have got into, but I got into it anyway, and realized my mistake. I lacked knowledge about what I could do to get out of that situation and I suffered the shame even though I knew it was not going anywhere, nor would it take me anywhere. While in it, apart from the traumas that I had to go through for emotional, financial, mental, and social abuse, I was ashamed of myself, yet I remained in it because I was thinking *what will the world say about me?* I have failed God and my church. How do I begin again? Who will listen to a person who has failed? Who will listen to me? I will be condemned, judged, and rejected (which happened anyway).

Those questions and worries crippled me, and instead of coming out, I suffered; even God had ordered me out. I had no choice when the person moved into a marriage with someone else. It was a hard situation to deal with, but I did, eventually, and prayerfully put the broken pieces of my life into God's hands, just like David wrote in Psalm 18. That was where the title FRESH START was inspired.

God made my life complete when I placed all the pieces before him. When I got my act together, he gave me a Fresh Start. Now, I'm alert to God's ways. I don't take God for granted. Every day I review the ways he works, and I try not to miss a thing. I feel put back together, and I'm watching my steps. God rewrote the text of my life when I opened the book of my heart to his eyes. Read Psalm 18:20

This book includes powerful insights and prayers that have helped people to transform their lives, breakthrough barriers to fulfilling their dreams and desires. I am sure it will help many to accomplish their goals to fulfil their purpose and potential. In fact, your testimony could be the next one I hear!

WHAT CAN STOP YOU?

Some things can hold you back from experiencing that Fresh Start:

> Fear
> Bitterness
> Unforgiveness
> Your perception of life
> Your past experiences
> Self-rejection and fear of rejection

It is not our circumstances that determine who we become, but how we handle them that leads to the fulfilment of destiny.

No matter what you have gone through, or maybe going through, believe it, other people have gone through worse and have not just survived but thrived. That should be a consolation and comfort for you.

THE CALL TO SALVATION

Fresh Starts with Life in Christ

Take a good look friends, at who you were when you got called into this life. Isn't it obvious that God deliberately chooses men and women that society overlooks and exploits and abuses, chooses these "nobodies" to expose the hollow pretensions of the "somebodies"? That makes it quite clear that none of you can get by with blowing your own horn before God. Everything that we have—positive thinking and positive living, a clean slate and a Fresh Start—comes from God by way of Jesus Christ. That's why we have the saying, "If you're going to blow a horn, blow a trumpet for God."1 Corinthians 1:26

WHY WILL GOD GRANT YOU A FRESH START?

To rewrite your story and turn your mess into a divine message. Somebody somewhere is going to be inspired and encouraged by your turnaround story. God does not waste. He wants to make you:

AN EXPERT, A COUNSELOR, A CONSULTANT, A LIFE COACH

Who comforts (consoles and encourages) us in every trouble (calamity and affliction), so that we may also be able to comfort (console and encourage) those who are in any kind of trouble or distress, with the comfort (consolation and encouragement) with which we are comforted (consoled and encouraged) by God. 2 Corinthians 1:4

That is my story. For instance, because I failed in making positive and wise marital decisions, God turned my story around for me to become a facilitator of destinies. By God's grace, my book *Divine Connections*, a premarital guide, and the program, *By the Well,* came out of that experience.

GOD USES YOUR ADVERSITY AS A SET-UP FOR YOUR COMEBACK!

"For though the righteous fall seven times, they rise again…" Proverbs 24:16,

In this life we experience a lot of put-downs, rejections, storms, disappointments, failures, losses, and bad relationships. Read PSALM 66:12.

PURPOSE

This book is for anyone who desires a change in their life story. It is for those who are tired of being in the same spot for years, in their relationships, marriage, career, ministry, or business, who desire to reach a new height of success or to break away from the failure of the past.

I carefully looked at the story of certain people who had a Fresh Start and noticed that for the most part they used the weapon of prayer along with other things to accomplish their goal. The purpose of this book is to help you to engage with the weapon of prayer to fast-track your Fresh Start. Jesus even attested to that:

"However, this kind does not go out except by prayer and fasting." Matthew 17:21

I always say that change will not happen except by prayer, depending on what you are asking for.

Prayer makes you vulnerable before God who is more than able to help you, according to Ephesians 3:20.

"Now to Him who is able to [carry out His purpose and] do superabundantly more than all that we dare ask or think [infinitely beyond our greatest prayers, hopes, or dreams], according to His power that is at work within us." Ephesians 3:20

And that was exactly what David did to obtain a Fresh Start. He spoke thus:

"God made my life complete when I placed all of the pieces of it before Him. When I cleaned up my act, He gave me a Fresh Start. Indeed, I've kept alert to God's ways and I haven't taken God for granted. Every day I review how He works and I try not to miss a thing. I feel put back together and I'm watching my step. God rewrote the text of my life when I opened the book of my heart to his eyes" (2 Samuel 22:21-25).

DAY 1

I AM MORE THAN THIS

PRAYER QUOTE:

"The presence of God is not imaginary; neither is prayer the indulgence of a delightful fancy... A purified and Spirit-controlled imagination is the sacred gift of seeing the ability to peer beyond the veil and gaze with astonished wonder upon the beauties and mysteries of things holy and eternal." -W. Tozer

SCRIPTURE:

"Then He said: "A certain man had two sons. And the younger of them said to his father, 'Father, give me the portion of goods that falls to me.' So, he divided to them his livelihood. And not many days after, the younger son gathered all together, journeyed to a far country, and there wasted his possessions with prodigal living.

But when he had spent all, there arose a severe famine in that land, and he began to be in want. Then he went and joined himself to a citizen of that country, and he sent him into his fields to feed swine. And he would gladly have filled his stomach with the pods that the swine ate, and no one gave him anything.

"But when he came to himself, he said, 'How many of my father's hired servants have bread enough and to spare, and I perish with hunger! I will arise and go to my father, and will say to him, "Father, I have sinned against heaven and before you, and I am no longer worthy to be called your son. Make me like one of your hired servants."'

"And he arose and came to his father. But when he was still a great way off, his father saw him and had compassion, and ran and fell on his neck and kissed him. And the son said to him, 'Father, I have sinned against heaven and in your sight, and am no longer worthy to be called your son.'

"But the father said to his servants, 'Bring out the best robe and put it on him and put a ring on his hand and sandals on his feet. And bring the fatted calf here and kill it and let us eat and be merry; for this my son was dead and is alive again; he was lost and is found.' And they began to be merry." (Luke 15:11-24)

The journey of Fresh Start usually starts with the sudden realization of our lost state, where we ought to be that we are not, or where we ought not to be but we are; what we ought to have that we don't have or what we have that we ought not to have.

God desires that we come back to our senses and the reality of who we are and our very potential whenever we make a mistake like the prodigal son in the above story.

Do not allow the past mistakes to define or determine your future, or even confine you. Also, do not allow your past successes to keep you from the best that is still ahead of you.

Fresh Start is a prophetic declaration of one who looks at himself and says, "Lord, I am thanking you for how far you have brought me but, I know you're not done with me yet. I still have a greater potential and capacity than what I am currently experiencing."

To experience a Fresh Start, you must come to the realization that beyond the limitations that surround you at present, there is still more that can be achieved. It's that point you come to conciousness that makes you aware that you can have a better life or condition than what you are currently experiencing. Jabez came to that point in his life. God spoke to me of Jabez's story, his was not a story of destitution or poverty because the phrase, "enlarge my coast", means I am doing something now, but, I want a larger impact and influence (1Chronicles 4:10). The curse upon him could have hindered him from achieving more but he was doing something with his life already. The fact that you're doing something does not mean you cannot climb higher or achieve much more. It dawned on Jabez that he could go higher.

You need to understand that beyond the struggle of today, there's a better life ahead; beyond the widowhood, divorce, separation, disappointment, bankruptcy, there's something positive waiting for you.

You may have all the right qualifications or certifications but not be in the right position, or have the right connections despite your experience. It's then that you need a Fresh Start.

You may have made several attempts to improve your situation - all ending in failure - and you are wondering if you are better than that. Just like Joseph, you can also have a Fresh Start. Joseph had a dream of becoming a leader but there was no actualization until thirteen years later after serving as a head slave, head prisoner, and at last the prime minister! (Genesis 37-41)

You may have miscalculated, mismanaged, and wandered into the pig slurp like the prodigal son, but there's hope if you can come back to your senses and place the pieces of your life back into His hands. We must always be aware that God is our father and He is ever waiting for us.

"For there is hope for a tree, If it is cut down, that it will sprout again, And that its tender shoots will not cease. Though its root may grow old in the earth, And its stump may die in the ground, Yet at the scent of water it will bud, And bring forth branches like a plant" (Job 14:7-9)

There is hope for you irrespective of your situation, be it financial, marital, or in any aspect of your life. Even if it appears that you have been cut down, as the fresh waters from heaven fall upon your life, you will sprout up again.

So, there should never be a time when you feel as though the end has come to your life or the level of success you have achieved is all there is to achieve. There is always more available for us once we are ready to believe God and launch out into the deep.

Scripture says in Jeremiah 31:2,

"Thus, says the Lord: The people who survived the sword found favor in the wilderness [place of exile] — when Israel sought to find rest." (They sought rest but found God.)

The desire we should have is to meet with God, and the encounter should transcend into reprogramming our lives for us to fit into His good plan. God has the power and He's willing to build us up again in all aspects of our lives that need rebuilding, irrespective of whatever we have lost.

There was a man called Mephibosheth who was meant for the palace but found himself living a low life. You might be in the same situation that he was, but be reminded that there is a God that can reverse the irreversible. (2 Samuel 9)

There is an intriguing part of the Scripture written by one of the wisest men who ever lived.

He said:

"There is an evil I have seen under the sun, As an error proceeding from the ruler: Folly is set in great dignity, While the rich sit in a lowly place. I have seen servants on horses, While princes walk on the ground like servants." (Ecclesiastes 10:5-7)

Solomon observed an unusual occurrence on the face of the Earth. He thought it was an error made by God. He saw folly being exalted while the blessed sat in low places; those who were to be in high places in life were in low places and he wondered about such an occurrence.

It is your season of moving from the dunghill into the palace of your destiny; your season of reversal of wrongs. God will restore dignity and respect to your life in Jesus' Name.

The story of Naman is a very interesting one as he was a General in the military whose capabilities were limited due to sickness. God terminated the rule of sickness and disease in his life and He can do the same for you. God can terminate all types of sickness even if is generational or terminal. It doesn't matter what plagues your health or denies you of a Fresh Start because Naman was given a new beginning and that same miracle will be replicated in your life. (2 Kings 5:1-10)

There is a promise for us in God's word that says: *"So, you shall serve the Lord your God, and He will bless your bread and your water. And I will take sickness away from the midst of you. No one shall suffer miscarriage or be barren in your land; I will fulfill the number of your days.* "(Exodus 23:25-26)

"I am more than this" represents the voice of a person who has experienced or is experiencing non-achievement, underachievement, failure, loss, devastation, and destitution. I am someone who seeks a greater height and expansion in life and who wants to make a greater impact on the lives of others.

For the Prodigal Son, the journey into the mess started with a bad decision, followed by reckless living and mismanagement. Once you know the source of your problem, a solution is not hard to find. So, if you're in bad shape right now, can you recollect how it all began, by calling on God you will not only know the genesis of your problem but the solution to it. (Jeremiah 33:3)

SOURCE OF PROBLEMS

Self-inflicted: The greatest source of problems affecting men today is the mess we create by ourselves. Many of us rebelled against God and were disobedient, making wrong choices with our financial management, choice of marital partner, and approach to raising our children, among other things.

"Before I was afflicted I went astray, but now your word do I keep [hearing, receiving, loving, and obeying it]." (Psalm 119:67)

Unprofitable friendships: Abraham could not experience advancement for some time because of the presence of Lot in his life. He entered a season of a FRESH START when he got rid of "LOT". Lot representing a person that was not meant to be with you in a seasoned life. The presence of Lot in Abraham's life impaired his vision, for God could not instruct him further until Lot left him. There could be one or more persons in your life that you may have to let go of your life to move forward. You must identify such in your life and make amends. (Genesis 12:5, Genesis 13:7)

Devil and his cohorts: This was the source of the problem that arose against Job. The Devil still seeks opportunities to infiltrate and destroy men's lives. (Job 1:8)

"For we do not wrestle against flesh and blood, but against principalities, against powers, against the rulers of the darkness of this age, against spiritual hosts of wickedness in the heavenly places." (Ephesians 6:12)

Accidental problems: Problems like these are negative occurrences that happen to us not because of a wrong we committed, but a fault arising from the error of another. An example would be a scenario where a marriage or business partner makes a wrong financial move that puts another innocent party under intense financial pressure, just like what the man Achan did despite God's warning to the children of Israel.

"Now Joshua said to Achan, "My son, I beg you, give

glory to the Lord God of Israel, and make confession to Him, and tell me now what you have done; do not hide it from me." And Achan answered Joshua and said, "Indeed I have sinned against the Lord God of Israel, and this is what I have done: When I saw among the spoils a beautiful Babylonian garment, two hundred shekels of silver, and a wedge of gold weighing fifty shekels, I coveted them and took them. And there they are, hidden in the earth in the midst of my tent, with the silver under it." (Joshua 7:19-21)

His singular action jeopardized the lives of an entire nation because he disobeyed a direct instruction from God.

It's time to acknowledge the fact that you are more than who you are right now.

YOU ARE MUCH MORE THAN THIS!

Fresh Start Gem: "We can never give up longing and wishing while we are thoroughly alive. There are certain things we need to feel to be beautiful and good, and we must hunger after them." - George Elliot

⚜

STRIVE TO BE THE BEST. GO AFTER THE BEST

PRAYER POINTS

- Father, thank you for granting me a Fresh Start and everything to live for, including a future in heaven. I praise you, Lord, the Alpha and the Omega, the Beginning and the End.

• Father, by your mercy have mercy on me for every way I have mismanaged or wasted resources you gave me including time, treasure, and talent. Restore me to my ordained position - spiritually, physically, mentally, emotionally, maritally, financially or ministerially, in the mighty name of Jesus (Isaiah 42:22)

• Father, empower me physically, spiritually, and financially for my Fresh Start and let the anointing for breakthroughs come upon me. Let every cycle of demotion and degradation be broken over my life and restore my dignity and honor (Isaiah 60)

• Father, I believe there is much more. Help me to achieve more than what I am currently experiencing. Make way for my elevation regardless of circumstances surrounding me right now (Isaiah 40:1-2)

• Father, because of your loving kindness and the redemptive work of Christ, enlarge my coast. Let your blessings manifest in my life. Help me break through every protocol and contrary policy (1 Chronicles 4:10)

ASSIGNMENT

• Write down those occurrences or mistakes that brought about setback or sorrow in your life.

• Write down areas in which you currently desire emancipation by God.

• Ensure that you take note of the instructions that the Holy Spirit will place in your heart to amend mistakes and to secure the desired emancipation.

DAY 2

✤

EMBRACING GREATER GLORY

PRAYER QUOTE:

"The greater the difficulty to be overcome, the more it will be seen to the glory of God how much can be done by Prayer and Faith." - George Muller

SCRIPTURE:

"I will bless the Lord at all times. His praise shall continually be in my mouth. My life makes its boast in the Lord. Let the humble and afflicted hear and be glad. O magnify the Lord with me and let us exalt His name together. I sought (inquired of) the Lord and required

Him [of necessity and on the authority of His Word], and He heard me, and delivered me from all my fears.

They looked to Him and were radiant. Their faces shall never blush for shame or be confused. This poor man cried, and the Lord heard him, and saved him out of all his troubles. The Angel of the Lord encamps around those who fear Him [who revere and worship Him with awe] and each of them He delivers. O taste and see that the Lord [our God] is good! Blessed (happy, fortunate, to be envied) is the man who trusts and takes refuge in Him."
Psalm 34:1-8 *AMP*

There is a God that secures greater glory for His children and He is still alive and working today. When you look unto him for a Fresh Start, He is more than able to ensure that you experience that which you desire from Him.

To experience a Fresh Start, you have to come to the realization that beyond the present level you're at in life, there are still many levels to be climbed, greater heights to be reached and greater exploits to manifest.

Jabez came to that realization when he was cursed at birth by his own mother and life became hard for a man that was destined to be more honorable than his siblings. When it dawned on him that he could have a better life, he prayed to the one who created him, and he received an opportunity for a better life. He embraced greater glory. I believe it was the same mindset that prompted Ruth, an accursed girl - not by anything she did wrong - but because she belonged to a cursed family and nation, to follow her mother-in-law to a foreign land in search of a better life.

Joseph was a man skilled in the interpretation of dreams, but he interpreted them for the wrong people in the wrong place. Yet, despite the adversity he faced, God still led him to his destiny, for the prison was not his destination, but the palace was, and God ensured that he got there and fulfilled his destiny. Beyond the struggles of today there is a better life ahead. Beyond widowhood, divorce, separation, disappointment, or loss of that significant person, there is a Fresh Start awaiting you.

You may have all the appropriate qualifications, degrees and certifications, but you're not in the right position or have the right connections in spite of your experience. You may have made several attempts to change your situation, all of which ended in failure, and you think, "Why? I'm better than this." Don't worry. Like Joseph, you can have that Fresh Start. You can experience the God of greater glory.

But the path of the [uncompromisingly] just and righteous is like the light of dawn, that shines more and more (brighter and clearer) until [it reaches its full strength and glory in] the perfect day [to be prepared]. Proverbs 4:18

The Scripture reveals that the path of one who has been made just by the blood of Jesus is illuminated with a light that shines in never-ending splendor. So, for those who put their faith in Christ Jesus there should never be a better yesterday. There is no better or worse, only better and best. Your life should advance from glory to glory.

"All of us! Nothing between us and God, our faces shining with the brightness of His face. And so, we are transfigured much like the Messiah, and our lives gradually become brighter and more beautiful as God enters our lives and we become like him." (2 Corinthians 3:18)

As you allow Jesus to direct your lives you shall experience more of God's glory radiating through, reaching into every aspect of your life including your finances, marriage, ministry, career, and business. You must know that God's plan and desire for you will always be greater and better, so if you are experiencing something contradictory in your life right now, it may be that it's the work of the enemy and you must resist and focus on what God desires you to experience (Jeremiah 29:11; James 4:7-8)

Have you, by miscalculation of time, wandered into the pig sty? There is hope if you can come back to your senses and place the pieces of your life into His hands as he is ever waiting.

"This is the way God put it. The Israelites found grace out in the desert; these people who survived the sword. Israelites, out looking for a place to rest, met God out looking for them! God told them, I'll never quit loving you. Expect love, love, and more love! And so now I'll start over with you and build you up again, dear virgin Israel. You: I'll resume your singing, grabbing tambourines and joining the dance. You: I'll go back to your old work of

planting vineyards on the Samaritan hillsides and sit back and enjoy the fruit. Oh, how I'll enjoy those harvests! The time is coming when watchmen will call out from the hilltops of Ephraim, "On your feet! Let's go to Zion; go to meet our God!" (Jeremiah 31:2)

The children of Israel were looking for a place of rest just like many of us who desire a place of rest today. They found God in their pursuit and He changed their story for the better, for as many as were obedient. God shall change your story in this season in the mighty name of Jesus.

A woman who suffered from haemorrhages knew she was more than a pawn in the hands of physicians and specialists and handed over her life to the one who could fix it. Because she had faith in God despite her difficulties, God gave her a Fresh Start and removed infirmity from her body. Thus, it was a Fresh Start for her when she received her healing after a long time of suffering. Could it be a sickness that has been the source of your sorrows and tears? God is willing to give you a Fresh Start today. (Luke 8:43-48)

Blind Bartimaeus knew that he was more than a beggar. He wanted his sight to be restored so that he could live a normal life and give up the practice of begging which was his profession. God is willing and able to bestow a miracle upon anyone who is willing to receive it, today. It may be that you have endured so much financial difficulty that you have been reduced to begging and seeking help from every source known to you. This may be due to lack of sight or ignorance which led you to make many wrong decisions. (Mark 10:46-52)

The woman by the well had better things to do with her body than selling it for sex. She had consorted with one man after another and the man she was with now was not her husband. She needed a Fresh Start and the mercy of God found her as she encountered the King of Glory. (John 4: 7-26)

Now consider the life of Jacob:

"Then Jacob was left alone and a man wrestled with him until the breaking of day. Now when He saw that He did not prevail against him, He touched the socket of his hip; and the socket of Jacob's hip was out of joint as He wrestled with him. And He said, "Let me go, for the day breaks." But he said, "I will not let you go unless you bless me!" So He said to him, "What is your name? He said, "Jacob." And He said, "Your name shall no longer be called Jacob, but Israel; for you have struggled with God and with men and have prevailed." (Genesis 32:24-28)

All his life, Jacob had been cheating people, but he knew he could be a better person. After several years of fleeing because he stole his brother's birth right, he was on his journey home when he had an encounter with an angel. Jacob wouldn't let the angel go unless he blessed him, so the angel changed his name from Jacob to Israel which signified a new dawn of glory.

The Prophet Ezekiel had a remarkable encounter:

*"The hand of the L*ORD* came upon me and brought me out in the Spirit of the* LORD *AND set me down during the valley, and it was full of bones. Then He caused me to pass by them all around, and behold, there were very many in the open valley, and indeed, they were very dry. And He said to me, "Son of man, can these bones live?" So, I answered, "O Lord G*OD*, you know." Again He said to me, "Prophesy to these bones, and say to them, 'O dry bones, hear the word of the L*ORD*! Thus says the Lord G*OD *to these bones: "Surely I will cause breath to enter into you, and you shall live. I will put sinews on you and bring flesh upon you, cover you with skin and put breath in you, and you shall live. Then you shall know that I am the L*ORD*. So I prophesied as I was commanded, and as I prophesied, there was a noise, and suddenly a rattling, and the bones came together, bone to bone. Indeed, as I looked, the sinews and the flesh came upon them, and the skin covered them over, but there was no breath in them. Also He said to me, "Prophesy to the breath, prophesy, son of man, and say to the breath, 'Thus says the Lord G*OD*: "Come from the four winds, O breath, and breathe on these slain, that they may live. So I prophesied as He commanded me, and breath came into them, and they lived, and stood upon their feet, an exceedingly great army."* (Ezekiel 37:1-10)

The dry bones had great potential but were trapped in that pit. Who would have known that such great potential was buried in that pit? We couldn't have known that those bones were going to become an exceedingly great army, but God proved himself mighty. Many of us have great potential but it's as though despite our efforts there is little fruit and manifestation of our labor to be seen. It looks as though we don't have any potential. However, God is ready and willing to showcase a greater glory. You will not only discover your hidden potentials or recover your dead or lost potential but the Almighty shall move you from obscurity to limelight in the mighty name of Jesus.

The once barren lady became the mother of a great man: that is another story of a great turn around, but it did not just happen; this woman prayed!

"So it came to pass in the process of time that Hannah conceived and bore a son, and called his name Samuel, saying, "Because I have asked for him from the Lord." Now the man Elkanah and all his house went up to offer to the Lord the yearly sacrifice and his vow. But Hannah did not go up, for she said to her husband, "Not until the child is weaned; then I will take him, that he may appear before the Lord and remain there forever." So Elkanah her husband said to her, "Do what seems best to you; wait until you have weaned him. Only let the Lord establish His word." Then the woman stayed and nursed her son until she had weaned him. Now when she had weaned him, she took him up with her, with three bulls, one ephah of flour, and a skin of wine, and brought him to the house of the Lord in Shiloh. And the child was young. Then they slaughtered a bull and brought the child to Eli. And she said, "O my lord! As your soul lives, my lord, I am the woman who stood by you here, praying

to the Lord. For this child I prayed, and the Lord has granted me my petition which I asked of Him. Therefore I also have lent him to the Lord; as long as he lives he shall be lent to the Lord." So, they worshiped the Lord there." (1 Samuel 1:20-28)

Hannah was more than a wife to Elkanah. She was a woman with the potential not just to be a mother, but one who would carry a great prophet; a king enthroner and king dethroner in her womb. She refused to give up until she bore that prophet. For her it was a Fresh Start when barrenness gave way to fruitfulness.

God is willing and able to bring you into an experience of greater glory as he activates a Fresh Start in your life. All you need is to embrace his loving and merciful offer. (Matthew 11:28-29)

Fresh Start gem: When obstacles arise, you change your direction to reach your goal, you do not change your decision to get there."

❃

TIME TO RUN TO GOD IS NOW!

PRAYER POINTS

• Father, I thank you, for it's my time for a Fresh Start as I embrace your glorious plan for my life and destiny (Psalm 31:15)

• Father, grant unto me insight and revelation that will make me progress from glory to glory in all areas of my life, show me Your ways, teach me Your paths. And guide me in Your truth in Jesus' name (Psalm 25:4-5)

• Father, grant unto me divine solutions to longstanding and recurring issues in my life and family that we may indeed enter into a season of Fresh Start. Grant me the power to rise above all negative circumstances. (Lack, barrenness, sickness, poverty, backwardness) (1 Kings 17:8-16; 2 Kings 4:1-7;5:1-14)

• Father, make way for me out of the wilderness (marital, financial, ministerial, vocational, and professional) and lead me into a land filled with milk and honey. Let every embargo, spiritual, or physical over my Fresh Start be lifted in the name of Jesus. (Psalm 24:7-10)

• I command everything that has hindered me from greatness to begin to give way now. "Red Sea" like the situation in my way, divide by fire now in the name of Jesus. Pharaoh standing in the way of my ordained and commanded Fresh Start, drown in the red sea in Jesus' Name (Exodus 14;15; Psalm 114)

ASSIGNMENT

• Write down recurring negative patterns in your life or family. Trust God for an encounter that will put an end to them.

DAY 3

❧

FORGETTING THE PAST

PRAYER QUOTE:

"Prayer is not overcoming God's reluctance but laying hold of God's willingness." - Martin Luther

SCRIPTURE:

"Though I also might have confidence in the flesh. If anyone else thinks he may have confidence in the flesh, I more so: circumcised the eighth day, of the stock of Israel, of the tribe of Benjamin, a Hebrew of the Hebrews; concerning the law, a Pharisee; concerning zeal, persecuting the church; concerning the righteousness which is in the law,

blameless. But what things were gain to me, these I have counted loss for Christ. Yet indeed I also count all things loss for the excellence of the knowledge of Christ Jesus my Lord, for whom I have suffered the loss of all things, and count them as rubbish, that I may gain Christ and be found in Him, not having my own righteousness, which is from the law, but that which is through faith in Christ, the righteousness which is from God by faith; that I may know Him and the power of His resurrection, and the fellowship of His sufferings, being conformed to His death, if, by any means, I may attain to the resurrection from the dead. Not that I have already attained, or am already perfected; but I press on, that I may lay hold of that for which Christ Jesus has also laid hold of me. Brethren, I do not count myself to have apprehended; but one thing I do, forgetting those things which are behind and reaching forward to those things which are ahead, I press toward the goal for the prize of the upward call of God in Christ Jesus. Therefore let us, as many as are mature, have this mind; and if in anything you think otherwise, God will reveal even this to you. Nevertheless, to the degree that we have already attained, let us walk by the same rule, let us be of the same mind." (Philippians 3:4-16)

That man had done several evil things in his life before he encountered that great light and Jesus spoke to him. He had actively participated in the killing of one of the church leaders. (Act 7:58)

Many people are caught up in the past, their lives centered on past successes or failures. Some took a wrong approach in raising their children, some lived wayward and promiscuous lives in times past, some made wrong decisions regarding their profession, others made mistakes in choosing a place to live. Some made the wrong financial decisions, buying a car they did not need, starting up a project without God's backing, making wrong business choices and so on. The man in the above passage from Philippians said he "pressed", meaning that there were so many oppositions that would hinder him but he was determined to forge ahead, despite the unpleasant situations and challenges that would stop him from advancing. And so, to enable your Fresh Start, one major characteristic you have to possess is the ability to press on regardless of your past.

The word press used in this context refers to taking aggressive action towards advancement, disregarding all hindrances that may get in the way. A quote from Myles Munroe states that "your future is not ahead of you, it's trapped within you."

Friend, you must come to know that the journey of your Fresh Start begins from within. It starts with an inward decision to choose to forget whatever may have occurred in the past. You may have made mistakes, done so many wrong things; You may have been lazy or foolish, but since God has chosen to remember us in His mercy, I also choose to embrace what He offers, and I commit myself to a forward march advancing into God's best plan for my life and so should you.

The story of Naomi and Ruth is one to consider when we discuss the issue of forgetting the past and looking forward to what's ahead.

"And Boaz said to the elders and all the people, "You are witnesses this day that I have bought all that was Elimelech's, and all that was Chilion's and Mahlon's, from the hand of Naomi. Moreover, Ruth the Moabitess, the widow of Mahlon, I have acquired as my wife, to perpetuate the name of the dead through his inheritance, that the name of the dead may not be cut off from among his brethren and from his position at the gate.* You are witnesses this day." And all the people who were at the gate, and the elders, said, "We are witnesses. The Lord make the woman who is coming to your house like Rachel and Leah, the two who built the house of Israel; and may you prosper in Ephrathah and be famous in Bethlehem. May your house be like the house of Perez, whom Tamar bore to Judah, because of the offspring which the Lord will give you from this young woman." So Boaz took Ruth and she became his wife; and when he went in to her, the Lord gave her conception, and she bore a son. Then the women said to Naomi, "Blessed be the Lord, who has not left you this day without a close relative; and may his name be famous in Israel! And may he be to you a restorer of life and a nourisher of your old age; for your daughter-in-law, who loves you, who is better to you than seven sons, has borne him." Then Naomi took the child and laid him on her bosom, and became a nurse to him. Also the neighbor women gave him a name, saying, "There is a son born to Naomi." And they called his name Obed. He is the father of Jesse, the father of David. Now

this is the genealogy of Perez: Perez begot Hezron; Hezron begot Ram, and Ram begot Amminadab; Amminadab begot Nahshon, and Nahshon begot Salmon;* Salmon begot Boaz, and Boaz begot Obed; Obed begot Jesse, and Jesse begot David." (Ruth 4:9-22)

In the days when judges ruled there was a man named Elimelech and Naomi was his wife. There was famine in the land, so he sojourned to Moab where he died and after his sons got married they also died, leaving their two wives behind as widows. Ruth and Oprah. Naomi decided to return to Israel and she resisted her two daughters-in-law from following her. Oprah turned back but Ruth was determined to follow her.

Naomi had lost her two sons and her husband. Ruth had lost her husband and she had no one else in her life except for her mother-in-law.

Both of them had faced such great difficulties in their life, so much so that when Naomi came back to Israel and arrived at Bethlehem, people came to embrace her, calling her Naomi, which meant pleasantness. She said, "don't call me Naomi, call me Mara," meaning bitterness.

She said, "I went out full and I came back empty. God has dealt bitterly with me." She didn't even consider Ruth whom she came back with. She said, "I came back empty. The sorrow was great."

Ruth herself was a Moabite maiden who was married to an Israelite who later died. She then found herself in a strange land with different customs away from all that was familiar to her. Both Naomi and Ruth needed to start their lives all over again. They began afresh, and God gave them both a Fresh Start. One major lesson we must learn from their lives is that they let go of the past. We saw in the Book of Ruth how Naomi and Ruth devised strategies for their physical wellbeing and ultimately for the advancement of their lives.

Ruth eventually married a very wealthy man named Boaz and she gave birth to a son named Obed and Obed begat Jesse and Jesse begat David. Jesus came from the lineage of David. What an amazing turnaround for a Moabite who had lost everything. She was brought into the Messianic Lineage as her life was turned around by the God of Fresh Start while Naomi had a daughter-in-law who was better to her than ten sons. I pray that God will turn your life around in this journey. I don't know why, but I love the Ruth and Boaz story very much.

Also, considering the life of Joseph we learn the principle of forgetting the past again:

> "Then Joseph could not restrain himself before all those who stood by him, and he cried out, "Make everyone go out from me!" So no one stood with him while Joseph made himself known to his brothers. And he wept aloud, and the Egyptians and the house of Pharaoh heard it. Then Joseph said to his brothers, "I am Joseph; does my father still live?" But his brothers could not

answer him, for they were dismayed in his presence. And Joseph said to his brothers, "Please come near to me." So they came near. Then he said: "I am Joseph your brother, whom you sold into Egypt. But now, do not therefore be grieved or angry with yourselves because you sold me here; for God sent me before you to preserve life. For these two years the famine has been in the land, and there are still five years in which there will be neither plowing nor harvesting. And God sent me before you to preserve a posterity for you in the earth, and to save your lives by a great deliverance. So now it was not you who sent me here, but God; and He has made me a father to Pharaoh, and lord of all his house, and a ruler throughout all the land of Egypt. "Hurry and go up to my father, and say to him, 'Thus says your son Joseph: "God has made me lord of all Egypt; come down to me, do not tarry. You shall dwell in the land of Goshen, and you shall be near to me, you and your children, your children's children, your flocks and your herds, and all that you have. There I will provide for you, lest you and your household, and all that you have, come to poverty; for there are still five years of famine." "And behold, your eyes and the eyes of my brother Benjamin see that it is my mouth that speaks to you. So you shall tell my father of all my glory in Egypt, and of all that you have seen; and you shall hurry and bring my father down here." Then he fell on his brother Benjamin's neck and wept, and Benjamin wept on his neck. Moreover he kissed all his brothers and wept over them, and after that his brothers talked with him." (Genesis 45:1-15)

Joseph was also a young gifted Israelite whom God gave a Fresh Start despite the wickedness that arose against him from his own household. His enemies were his own blood, but God gave him victory. When you read the speech that he gave his brothers, after he had already risen into God's plan and purpose for his life, you'll see that he wasn't one who held grudges against them because that would have kept him in the past and he wouldn't have been able to launch into God's best plan for his life. He ignored the sorrows that plagued his life which first began in his own household. He was thrown into a pit, sold as a slave, tempted to fornicate but resisted, was lied upon, thrown into prison, and finally moved to the palace.

God will move you into the palace of your destiny in this season of Fresh Start in Jesus' Name.

Many of us have been experiencing non-achievement, underachievement, failure, loss, devastation and destitution. While some of us need to reach greater heights, expand our life plan to achieve greater impact, and better results, God will grant all our heart's desires in this season of Fresh Start.

What may have hindered many of us in time past may have been mistakes we made, bad decisions, negligence, or other people's mistakes, just like a man called Mephibosheth, a grandson of King Saul (2 Samuel 4:4).

DO NOT ALLOW THE BITTERNESS OF THE PAST TO HOLD YOU BACK FROM THE GLORIOUS FUTURE AHEAD OF YOU!

Just as God wants us to forget the past he also desires that we advance into the future, and as mentioned earlier, this starts from within. You can be better than who you are now. You can achieve more for your life than what you are currently experiencing. (Isaiah 43:18-19)

To advance into the future you will need to:

• Have a clear and well-defined purpose and focus. If you change your focus, you can have a Fresh Start.

• Avoid distractions. There will be several distractions that will come your way and derail your focus, but you must note them and avoid them. Remember anything that's not on your God-given path is a distraction.

• Pay no attention to contrary voices and crowds. Even Naomi did not want Ruth to proceed with her, not because she meant to harm but because she thought that was the right thing to do. You must know what God wants you to do and take the steps He wants you to take. You shouldn't seek to follow the crowd but rather be led by God's spirit. However, this doesn't mean that you shouldn't seek advice from others who are more experienced or have had success in the area you seek to embark upon.

• Take hold of opportunities as they come. *"But time and chance happen to them all."* (Ecclesiastes

9:11) Opportunities will always come up as it's a law from Heaven. Take advantage of them by preparing ahead. You might not see clouds or rain but just prepare. There could be a fresh, cleansing rain ahead.

• Be disciplined and exercise control over your desires and inordinate cravings; discipline in an area of timing, food, relationships, sex, and hobbies. Lack of discipline and self -control has destroyed many, so be careful.

• Seek knowledge. No knowledge is wasted, but you don't have time to get all the knowledge available to mankind. Look for relevant knowledge and immediately seek its application. Knowledge on its own cannot do much unless it is applied. Let go of pride, be persistent, and pay attention to your choices. (Be led by the Spirit. Remember to be spiritually minded is life and peace. Romans 8:6). Have a vision and direction, audaciously take risks, and please be patient but not sluggish.

Also Note:

Success is not comparing. Avoid comparison with others. It will save you from undue pressure. (2 Corinthians 10:12)

The prodigal son decided on an action plan. Trust God to help you decide on one today. (Luke 15: 18-19)

Set a goal and ensure it's **SMART**: Specific, Measurable, Attainable, Realistic, and Timely.

Fresh Start Gem: "The past is dead except for the life you give it."- Myles Munroe

❀

LET GO AND LET GOD!

PRAYER POINTS

• Father, I thank you for the great future you have in store for me. I magnify your name for this season of Fresh Start. Father, let the water of affliction stop flowing in my life; rescue my life from all manner of trouble, for You are my redeemer. (Psalm 34)

• Father, detach from me everything tying me down to the past; cut me off from such bondage in Jesus' Name. I'm struggling; please help me to forget the past and grant me the grace to embrace the new. (Isaiah 43:18-19; Isaiah 54:1-8)

• Father, inspire me to prepare to seize the opportunities that will arise in my nearest future. Empower me for a new beginning and grant me the grace to receive and embrace it. (Proverbs 2:10-11; Psalm 32:8; Isaiah 30:21)

• Father, I place the totality of my life in your hands. Put the broken pieces together and rewrite my history and that of my family; do a new thing for us in Jesus' Name. (Jeremiah 31:3-4)

• Father let every good thing the past has taken away from me return in greater measure in this season of Fresh Start. (Isaiah 42:22; Joel 2:23-25)

ASSIGNMENT

• Write out all your vision and goals. Where do you want to be in 12 months? What do you want to see?

Take note of specific areas you need to develop and work on in preparation for the opportunities that will arise as a result of this Fresh Start.

DAY 4

✻

STRATEGIC REPOSITIONING

PRAYER QUOTE:

"Prayer is when you talk to God; meditation is when you listen to God." - Diana Robinson

Strategic refers to relating to the identification of long-term or overall aims and interests, and the means of achieving them. It's a carefully designed plan to serve a particular purpose or advantage relating to the gaining of overall or long-term pursuit.

Reposition: to place in a different position; to adjust or alter. Altering a given position based on the long-term goal.

When we talk of strategic repositioning we are referring to a deliberate and conscious effort by an individual to place themselves into the future of their changing circumstances and environment; plugging themselves into the future destined for them. Ruth the Moabite was one person that plugged herself into a future that was beyond her. She started out as a foreign widow but ended up as the wife of a rich head of a conglomerate and not just that, it placed her name with the genealogy of Jesus Christ. You might not know, but God knows. (Isaiah 46:10)

RELOCATION

Abraham needed a Fresh Start. God knew that his present location would hinder him from moving into all that God had in store for him. Therefore, he had to be physically moved. (Genesis 12:1-5)

God desired that Abraham lead a great nation, but first, he told him to relocate. Many of us must reposition ourselves if we ever want to experience the Fresh Start that God desires for us. When we talk about strategic repositioning, it's something that deals with God's overall plan for us. There's a backend somewhere and you might not know where but there is a strategy to get to it. The Bible says in Isaiah:

"Remember the former things of old, For I am God, and there is no other; I am God, and there is none like me, Declaring the end from the beginning, And from ancient times things that are not yet done, saying, 'My counsel shall stand, And I will do all my pleasure," (Isaiah 46:9-10)

If you have a building goal of any sort, you know what you want to achieve. You have envisioned the big picture but to manifest it, you assemble architects, engineers and the likes to fulfill your project. Some people will arrive to help at different times and then they may leave. They may not know what your vision for the finished project is because they come into that project at different times to carry out their own assignment. Everyone does their bit until the structure is whole and visible.

We are likened to a building in God's hands. He knows the end result that we don't know but that things are happening and falling into place that will deliver us to that end. Part of the journey might be troublesome or hard, but we must rest assured that the outcome will be glorious. God's plan is a careful design or plans to serve a particular purpose or advantage relating to the gaining of overall or long-term accomplishment.

Repositioning refers to placing yourself in a different position from where you are. It could be for behavioral, physical, mental, emotional, and marital reasons, amongst others, but the purpose for the repositioning is a greater blessing.

I have witnessed things changing for people after their physical relocation. You may have to move from a position of comfort to an entirely new place for your desired change to occur. I was recently in a meeting and was told that for me to break through to the next level in my field of employment, that I must break away from my present circle of associates.

Remember, Scripture says that:

"Eye has not seen, nor ear heard, Nor have entered into the heart of man. The things which God has prepared for those who love Him." (1 Corinthians 2:9)

There are great things already prepared for those who love God, so there will be alterations required as well as strategic relocation for us to access that which He desires for our lives.

"Now the LORD had said to Abram: "Get out of your country, From your family and from your father's house, To a land that I will show you. I will make you a great nation; I will bless you. And make your name great; And you shall be a blessing. I will bless those who bless you, And I will curse him who curses you; And in you all the families of the earth shall be blessed." (Genesis 12:1-5)

Strategic Repositioning Will Sometimes Involve:

RELOCATION

God promised to make Abram a great nation, but he had to leave the place he was in and reposition himself to activate God's blessing upon his life. Abram had to leave Haran to fulfill his destiny to become the father of many nations.

Ruth had to move from Moab to Judah. (Ruth 1) I know that we often don't want to leave what is familiar for the unfamiliar or what is comfortable for that which may be uncomfortable like the Hebrews did (Numbers 11:4-6). God will allow some doors to close even if we try to forcefully open them, and we may not understand why, but if we let God have His perfect way, the end result shall be glorious. (James 1:4-8)

SEPARATION

There may be a need for separating from your family or certain relationships that you may be in because they're not going to help you with your Fresh Start.

When God is activating a restructuring in your life, you may not know it. God may separate you from certain people for him to carry out his counsel over your life. Even though Abraham went with Lot, his nephew, there came a time when God had to separate them. "Lot" represents an unnecessary attached person in your destiny journey. When God asked Abraham to move, the instruction was not to go with anybody but he went with Lotand had to separate from him at a point due to differences that occur between their staffs. (Genesis 13) Abraham did not get any further instruction until after their separation.

Some people may have been good to you in the past but because they may not fit into your Fresh Start, you may need to let go of them. That may be painful, but you must let go.

There was a time in my life when I was convinced that I needed a Fresh Start because I'd come to the realization that I was making motions without movement. While contemplating this, I received a message from the

Holy Spirit that I wouldn't know what the next step was except that I was to be separated from "Lot". Although unknown to me at that time, "Lot" was a person I shouldn't have been in a relationship with. While waiting, because I didn't know what to do or how to go about it, God made this person of interest go by force because he went to marry someone else. In that instance, I didn't have a choice, other than to move on with the broken pieces of my life that I had to place in God's hand and He has turned that mess into a divine message. Out of that mess came a book, *Divine Connections*, and a program called *By The Well*. Both the book and program are helping the singles to secure and protect their destiny before saying I do.

There are also certain habits that you may have to do away within your life, which if you don't deal with would hinder you from going to the next level. It may not be easy though, but when that trimming is on-going, those are the times we are feeling the hardness and it looks as if we are suffering. These are pruning seasons. (The negativity, indiscipline, procrastination, slothfulness, impatience, mindset, and so on) For instance, I had to get past my procrastination and slothfulness to complete this project.

You may also need to detach yourself from traditions of men. What you need is insight and divine direction to know what exactly what to do to move on with life. It may not have always been, but hey, who says God cannot start something new with you. And the insight and direction you need is released to you now in Jesus

Name. (2 Corinthians 6: 11-13, Coll 2: 21-23).

Many destinies have been frustrated and truncated by the politics and policies of this world – family traditions, church doctrines that are just mere men's interpretations, societal expectations such in the case of Leah and Rachel. (That the older sibling must marry before the junior. This was what led to the marital complications in the life of Jacob's family (Genesis 29:26). That may have stopped some people, but don't give into such, lean on the direction of God (Proverbs 3:5-6) For me the question is always, "What is the Lord saying."

God has an agenda for your life and he is repositioning you for greatness and all-around blessings. For this day, the emphasis is on the book of Ruth, as we consider the story of the young Moabites, Ruth went through a lot of hardships.

She was strategically placed in the genealogy of Jesus as she rose into God's purpose for her life, embracing a Fresh Start. Many of us may not understand the happenings in our lives now, but in some few years to come we would grasp the reasons behind the situations we faced. In years to come they would begin to understand like Joseph why they went to prison, why they had to meet the butler, why they had to go to Potiphar's house, why some doors are closed. That's when many will begin to connect the dots in their lives and understand the strategies that God used.

We must not forget that the scripture says:

"[Earnestly] remember the former things, [which I did] of old; for I am God, and there is no one else; I am God, and there is none like Me, Declaring the end and the result from the beginning, and from ancient times the things that are not yet done, saying, My counsel shall stand, and I will do all My pleasure and purpose, Calling a ravenous bird from the east—the man [Cyrus] who executes My counsel from a far country. Yes, I have spoken, and I will bring it to pass; I have purposed it, and I will do it." (Isaiah 46:9-11)

Once God speaks, He is determined to bring his word to pass in our lives. He has said that his word shall not come back void but accomplish that which he pleases. It's essential that we know that before God commences any endeavor, he has already declared the end. To us it might look as though we are just beginning, but to him it's a finished work already. All that remains is for us to reposition ourselves and align.

The Psalmist cried:

"Listen to my prayer, O God, and hide not yourself from my supplication! Attend to me and answer me; I am restless and distraught in my complaint and must moan As for me, I will call upon God, and the Lord will save me. Evening and morning and at noon will I utter my complaint and moan and sigh, and He will hear my voice". (Psalm 55:1-2, 16-17 AMPC)

We might not know what God is preparing for us, but he knows, and it's left to us to reach out to him in prayer to find out that which he has in mind concerning our lives. We might have done all that we know to do.

The question is, have we heard from God?

Hearing from God is one of the most important keys when it comes to securing a Fresh Start. (1 Corinthians 2 :9-12; Romans 8: 14)

When the bible says eye has not seen nor heard it means that our spiritual sense must be alert through focus. To receive what cannot be gotten in the natural.

God is a spirit, and anyone that would be led by him, or repositioned by him must seek to connect to him by the spirit. That is why we are engaging in these 21 days of Prayers, seeking his face for a Fresh Start.

DIFFERENT KINDS OF REPOSITIONING

- Mental Repositioning.

- Spiritual Repositioning

- Emotional

- Physical

- Financial

- Marital

WHY DO YOU NEED REPOSITIONING?

- To Fulfill God's Agenda For Your Destiny

- For Greatness

- For Honor

- For Fulfilment

- For divine Connections

- For Blessings

- For Restoration

A classic case is that of Ruth found in the book of Ruth chapters 1-4. In her conclusion of the life story, we found her in the genealogy of Jesus Christ.

Let's not forget her mentor who had to relocate. In conclusion it was written of her, *"Now at last Naomi has a son again."* Ruth 4:17

To secure the reposition you need, you must be passionate.

"And Ruth said, Urge me not to leave you or to turn back from following you; for where you go I will go, and where you lodge I will lodge. Your people shall be my people and your God my God. Where you die I will die, and there will I be buried. The Lord do so to me, and more also, if anything but death parts me from you." (Ruth 1:16-17)

You might have been held bound, but as God is repositioning you for Fresh Start. Your destiny will be released into its fullness in this season. Every embargo or limitation saying no to your repositioning for the fulfillment of your destiny they are removed in Jesus Name.

Fresh Start Gem: "Destiny is not for comfort seekers. Destiny is for the daring and determined who are willing to endure some discomfort, delay, gratification, and go where destiny leads," -T.D Jakes

※

BE DARING. BE BOLD. BE A RISK TAKER!

PRAYER POINTS

• Father, thank you for the gift of life and the opportunity given to me for a Fresh Start. Let your mercy prevail over judgment in my life (James 2:13)

• Father, please if wrongfully located, relocate me by force, if wrongfully in any relationship divinely separate me, if wrongly controlled and directed by doctrines, traditions, and policies please help me to redirect (Psalms 37:23)

• Father, the Ancient of Days, the ones that declare the end from the beginning, please help me to make the right decisions and choices that will usher me into my FRESH START season. As I do, please help me to pursue the necessary course of action with passion. I may not know what, I may not know how, I may not when, but I trust you for my future. (Proverbs 3:5-6; Psalms 32:8)

• Father, please let me hear your voice with precision and clarity at this very season of change. (Romans 8:14; Isaiah 30:21;1 Corinthians 2:9-12)

- Father, in your mercy, strategically position me to connect with every benefactor of my Fresh Start and helpers of destiny. Grant me the grace to recognize, acknowledge and accept them; disconnect me from wasters and distracters. In Jesus' name I prayed and to You father, I give all the glory.

ASSIGNMENT

- Think. Write. Act.

- What habits must be broken?

- What relationships have to go?

- What places cannot be visited?

DAY 5

✣

TOTAL SURRENDER

PRAYER QUOTE:

"Prayer fills man's emptiness with God's fullness, Prayer puts away man's poverty with God's riches. Prayer puts away man's weakness with the coming of God's strength. It banishes man's littleness with God's greatness." - E.M Bounds

SCRIPTURE:

"Now it came to pass after these things that God tested Abraham, and said to him, "Abraham!"And he said, "Here I am." Then He said, "Take now your son, your only son Isaac, whom you love, and go to the land of Moriah, and offer him there as a burnt offering on one of the mountains of which I shall tell you." So Abraham rose

early in the morning and saddled his donkey, and took two of his young men with him, and Isaac his son; and he split the wood for the burnt offering, and arose and went to the place of which God had told him. Then on the third day Abraham lifted his eyes and saw the place afar off. And Abraham said to his young men, "Stay here with the donkey; the lad and I will go yonder and worship, and we will come back to you." So Abraham took the wood of the burnt offering and laid it on Isaac his son; and he took the fire in his hand, and a knife, and the two of them went together. But Isaac spoke to Abraham his father and said, "My father!" And he said, "Here I am, my son." Then he said, "Look, the fire and the wood, but where is the lamb for a burnt offering?" And Abraham said, "My son, God will provide for Himself the lamb for a burnt offering." So the two of them went together. Then they came to the place of which God had told him. And Abraham built an altar there and placed the wood in order; and he bound Isaac his son and laid him on the altar, upon the wood. And Abraham stretched out his hand and took the knife to slay his son." (Genesis 22:1- 10)

God asked Abraham to take his son, the only son whom he loved, to go and sacrifice him as a burnt offering, and he obeyed God. Then God aroused and blessed him.

"Then the Angel of the Lord called to Abraham a second time out of heaven, and said: "By Myself I have sworn, says the Lord, because you have done this thing, and have not withheld your son, your only son. Blessing I will bless

you and multiplying I will multiply your descendants as the stars of the heaven and as the sand which is on the seashore; and your descendants shall possess the gate of their enemies. In your seed all the nations of the earth shall be blessed, because you have obeyed My voice." (Genesis 22:15-19)

Yesterday, we talked and prayed about STRATEGIC REPOSITIONING, and today we shall be talking about TOTAL SURRENDER. It takes a person who has totally surrendered to yield to repositioning. Who says it is easy? But to experience FRESH START, total surrender is necessary.

What is total surrender and to whom do you surrender? To surrender means to give in, yield, and submit to authority, and authority in this instance is the Almighty God. Borrowing some words from William McDonald's song, "I surrender all to you, everything I give to You, withholding nothing, withholding nothing."

It means you're saying to God, whatever you are telling me, whether I believe it or not, I'll do it. It may be comfortable, it may not. I may not understand how giving up my last groceries to save another person's life will turn my life around, so much so that I will end up having ceased the flow of provisions in the recession. Or how I, at the verge of repossession, will suddenly have a surplus that will sustain me for the rest of my life.

Honestly, they don't make sense, but Lord I surrender

to your will, whatever, wherever, whenever, however, and with whomever, I'm ready to go by your instruction to enter into my Fresh Start. (1 Kings 17:8-16;2 Kings 4:1-7)

Because Abraham was willing to totally surrender, and he did not struggle with God. He was blessed beyond description. The bible says in Hebrews

"For when God made a promise to Abraham, because He could swear by no one greater, He swore by Himself, "Surely blessing I will bless you, and multiplying I will multiply you." (Hebrews 6:13-15)

He obtained such an order of blessings as a result of his obedience and surrender to God's will. To secure your Fresh Start you will need to surrender the entirety of your will, intellect, and emotions to him.

The journey of Fresh Start is enhanced by active and prompt obedience to instructions regardless of your understanding or not. It may sound illogical or even unreasonable, but just do it anyway. I remember a funny story that happened some time ago, a very good friend of mine approached me to report God to me, that things were not working well for him then.

Anyway, I went to God on his behalf and God gave me the Word for him, from 2 Kings 3:16-17 "This dry valley will be filled with pools of water! You will see neither wind nor rain, says the LORD, but this valley will be filled with water." In other words, he should not worry, things may not go as expected, but he will not lack anything good, and truly God sustained him through the period.

Fresh Start Gem: "The opportunity is in the problem, the moment I see a problem, I immediately begin to think about the opportunities that can be created by trying to solve it." - Strive Masiyiwa.

✤

FOR YOUR NEXT LEVEL; FIRST OFF LOOK INWARD!

PRAYER POINTS

• Father, I thank you for giving me the opportunity to partake in this opportunity for a Fresh Start. You are the Omniscient, I absolutely surrender to you, let thy will be done in my life.

• Father, have mercy in any way that I'm short of total surrender to You and Your will in any form. Any practice of mine working against my Fresh Start, let it be truncated, take away stubbornness from my heart in Jesus name (2 Corinthians 10:6; 1 Samuel 15:22)

• I refuse to be disobedient to divine visions and instructions for my Fresh Start, even when not fully understanding the full implication of such. (Acts 26:19)

• Father, grant me the grace to take the very steps required to enter into my Fresh Start; "Thy will be done." (Luke 22:42)

• Father, help me to be swift to hear, remove confusion from my life, show me the path of life according to the WORD and plan for my life in the mighty name of Jesus (James 1:19-27)

ASSIGNMENT

• Write down areas of your life that the Holy Spirit has ministered to you to let go of and surrender to him; take definite action.

DAY 6

✤

STRATEGIC PURSUIT

PRAYER QUOTE:

"If God's word says He hears and answers prayers, and if that Word doesn't depart before your eyes, then you are bound to see yourself with the things you asked for. If you don't see yourself with the things you asked for, if you don't see yourself with the things you desire, then God's Word has departed from before your eyes." - Kenneth Hagin

SCRIPTURE:

"Then Naomi her mother-in-law said to Ruth, My daughter, shall I not seek rest or a home for you, that you may prosper?² And now is not Boaz, with whose maidens you were, our relative? See, he is winnowing barley tonight at the threshing floor. Wash and anoint yourself

therefore, and put on your best clothes and go down to the threshing floor, but do not make yourself known to the man until he has finished eating and drinking. But when he lies down, notice the place where he lies; then go and uncover his feet and lie down. And he will tell you what to do. And Ruth said to her, All that you say to me I will do. So she went down to the threshing floor and did just as her mother-in-law had told her." (Ruth 3:1-6)

To Pursue is to chase after somebody or something to catch, attack, or overtake. You can call it striving to obtain or achieve something overtime – a goal, vision, dream, or purpose. It is pressing forward to fulfill an agenda. (Philippians 3:12-14)

It is making aggressive and unrelenting efforts in recovering what has been lost or to obtain something that you know is yours, but has been taken over by another, like in the case of David (1 Samuel 30). Upon discovering his loss, David inquired of the LORD, "Shall I pursue this troop? Shall I overtake them? (1 Samuel 30:7-8) He was told, "Pursue, for you shall surely overtake them, and without fail recover all." And it was recorded that, "David recovered all."

That was power and result of the pursuit. From both Ruth's and David's story, one can conclude that you need a divine strategy in the pursuit of your Fresh Start.

It's important that you employ the wisdom and strategies of heaven in seeking your desired Fresh Start. In the earlier text we see how Naomi gave Ruth a definite plan and guide to secure her desired Fresh Start, and this is a very important insight that you should consider and learn from.

Stop dwelling on the pain life's occurrences might have caused you, you must let go of the pain and reach out to new beginnings that God is offering you. So, stop staring at the closed door; it will prevent you from seeing the new door. We must learn to say bye to pain and sorrow. I love this song, I believe it goes thus, "So long bye, bye. Bye, bye to my pain and sorrow..." By Jonathan Nelson.

"Forget the former things; do not dwell on the past. See, I am doing a new thing! Now it springs up; do you not perceive it? I am making a way in the wilderness and streams in the wasteland." (Isaiah 43:18-19)

- **Be prayerful**: It's important that you sustain a habitual prayer life. It might not be easy to develop at first, but as you obey and yield your vessels you would see yourself walking in such reality. It is major as it would help you sustain your Fresh Start. If you don't have a prayer lifestyle, this program will set you on course. It is understood that whatever habit you engage in for 21 days becomes habitual.

- **Be focused**. Avoid distractions. There are so many things that would want to shift your gaze off your desired Fresh Start, you must learn to ignore any form of distractions and focus on the mark set before you. (Hebrews 12:1-2; 2 Kings 2: 1-18)

- **You must be rugged.**

- **You must be passionate.**

- **Have a goal**: Having a fixed goal is vital in securing our Fresh Start. It's impossible to actualize anything of value without having a goal in mind. It spurs you to stretch and reach out for more.

- **Know who you are**: Know what you were designed to do or become. Don't try to become someone else, but be who God wants you to be.

- **Know what you want**: When we come to God in prayer, it's essential that we are definite with our request; it will help us know when our prayers have been answered. (Ruth 1:14-15)

- **Be consistent**: Consistency is key because it leads to mastery in a particular endeavor.

- **Be disciplined**: Discipline entails denying one's self of what's convenient to achieve what's needed.

- **Be focused**: Focus is also very important in securing our Fresh Start, as it helps us channel all our energy to produce a certain outcome or result.

- **Be generous**: Invest in acts of charity. Charity yields high returns. Don't hoard your goods; spread them around.

- **Be a blessing to others**. This could be your last night. When the clouds are full of water, it rains. When the wind blows down a tree, it lies where it falls. Don't sit there watching the wind. Do your own work. Don't stare at the clouds. Get on with your life. Just as you'll never understand the mystery of life forming in a pregnant woman, you'll never understand the mystery at work in all that God does. Go to work in the morning and stick to it until evening without watching the clock. You never know from moment to moment how your work will turn out in the end.

Other important advice on strategies are:

- Invest in your life; invest in others

- Have a mentor

- Be expectant

- Be a mentor

- Be friendly

- Pursue knowledge

- Be innovative

- Be creative.

- Make sure you Network

- Follow your passion

- Be adaptable

- Be patient

- Look forward, not backward

Life is all about the choices that we make, so it's important we make the right ones, not give in to frivolities or decisions that will lead to failure.

Ruth decided to stay and follow through into an unknown future while Orpah took the easy way out. Ruth's decision brought her into a glorious future. We do not know the outcome of Orpah's decision, but what we do know is that Orpah was not in the lineage of Jesus, but Ruth was.

Abraham was called out of Haran to an unknown land, to the place of his blessing; but, Isaac was instructed to stay behind in recession while being blessed. When making decisions, one thing is needful, be sure you are led by the Spirit. Obedience following instruction will secure us our Fresh Start.

Remember what Mary told the servants at the wedding:

His mother said to the servants, "Whatever He says to you, do it." (John 2:5)

Your Fresh Start may be hidden in helping others, we should be willing to lend help to people we meet. Ruth was not selfish but selfless, because she was determined to help mother-in-law and in the process she connected the dots to her own destiny; a helpful person that extends hands today may turn out to be someone who continues to help us or be of help to our children tomorrow.

Choose to see the best in every situation that comes

your way. Prison may have been a hard place, but it was a strategic place for Joseph's come back and the beginning of the journey to the fulfillment of a long-time dream.

Fresh Start Gem: "As long as we are persistent in our pursuit of our deepest destiny. We will continue to grow. We cannot choose the day or time when we will fully bloom. It happens in its own time." - Denis Waitley

✢

**HAVE A PLAN OF ACTION.
RELENTLESSLY PURSUE IT!**

PRAYER POINTS

• Father, thank you for this journey you have started in me and through me. I'm grateful for the grace that got me saved and for the attached privileges like a FRESH START. (Ephesians 2:8-9:3:12;Colossians.1:12)

• Father, grant me the grace to forge ahead: Help me to let go of the past.

• Father, grant me the wisdom and the power to intelligently and diligently pursue what is rightfully mine, that I may regain all that I have lost ignorantly, or by negligence (Matthew 11:12; James 1:5)

• I come against the operation and activity of the spirit of apathy, lethargy, procrastination, slothfulness, and complacency that could affect or stop my strategic pursuit. In the name of Jesus. (Proverbs 1:32; 13:4; Zephaniah 1:12; 1 Corinthians 9:24-27)

• I come against every arrow of discouragement, doubt, delay, distraction, diversion, depression and defeat in the pursuit of my Fresh Start. I command such arrows to backfire in the mighty name of Jesus (Psalm 11:2; Proverbs 13:12; Numbers 13:26-33)

ASSIGNMENT

• Pray in the Holy Ghost for 3 hours today and Write down insights and inspirations for definite strategies you would take for your FRESH START.

DAY 7

⚜

THE SET TIME

PRAYER QUOTE:

"Praying in tongues charges your spirit like a battery charger charges a battery." - Kenneth Hagin

SCRIPTURE:

"You will arise and have mercy and loving-kindness for Zion, for it is time to have pity and compassion for her; yes, the set time has come (the moment designated)." (Psalm 102:13)

Yesterday was about strategic pursuit. It takes a person who is sure it is their time to stubbornly, aggressively, persistently pursue the opportunity for their Fresh Start.

Certain people know that there is a set time for their comeback and bouncing back from whatever low level they may have fallen into. For instance, this person speaking here recognized their set time and was now talking to God saying, "Lord have mercy on us, for it is time to have pity on us." Even if that time has not been said or pronounced specifically, this man was saying that it is time to have pity on us, saying yea the set time has come. It was a request and affirmation.

A set time is an opportune time for something significant to happen. It is an appointed time. It is a time for fulfillment of a promise. It is a designated moment; it is a specified time for something spectacular to happen according to the plans and agenda of God. It is a time set aside for God to act for or against someone. (Ps.12:5; 119:126). It's an appointed time of fulfillment of the promise, like someone saying, "I knew that God, you have told me 400 years ago that these things would happen, that I would get out of bondage. You have told me that after seventy years I must cry and now I am sensing that it's my set time. You have told me that after I have suffered a while I would move into something new, that you would perfect me, settle me, and establish the works of my hands, that you would do some great things in my life. Now I am sensing it and he went back to God and said, "Lord it's time to have pity and compassion on me because it's the moment you have designated for me, not referring to my own moment. But the moment you have designated. (Psalm 98:3 Jeremiah 29:10-13; Daniel 9; Genesis 15:13 -16; Exodus 3)

It's also a time set apart by God to act for you and against your opposition. (Exodus 3:7-10; Isaiah 49:23-26)

You must have expectations when you come to God for your FRESH START. Without expectation there cannot be any manifestation. When the woman with the issue of blood who came to Jesus for her healings in Mark 5, was coming to Jesus, there was an expectation that this is my set time for recovery, so she knew what she was in for and she went after it. When blind Bartimaeus had the opportunity at his disposition, he must have said to himself, I cannot miss this time no matter what was going on around me. He was focused because that was his set time and he recognized it. To enter into your Fresh Start you must be able to perceive your season. I perceived it is my set time and I believe you know too and that is why you have this book in your hand right now. I'm praying that you will not miss it in Jesus' mighty name.

"To everything there is a season, and a time for every matter or purpose under heaven." (Ecclesiastes 3:11)

There is a time to go through adversity and time to advance; there is a time for trouble to end. Since there is a termination date, there has to be a starting date. This is your starting day!

There is a time for vision to be birthed again, there is a time for vision to be delivered, and there is time for manifestation.

"(Even the migratory birds are punctual to their seasons.)

Yes, the stork (excelling in the great height of her flight) in the heavens knows her appointed times (of migration), and the turtledove, the swallow, and the crane observe the time of their return. But My people do not know the law of the Lord (which the lower animals instinctively recognize in so far as it applies to them)." (Jeremiah 8:7)

If birds know, then how much more do we need to see. We also must know and we must have a sense of time knowing what to do. In a set time there is remembrance.

We also have our responsibility and its payback. You might think that I don't know anybody, Mephibosheth never thought David would remember him. He was four years old when he was crippled, he might not have even known David. Mephibosheth was Jonathan's son, he might not have even known that his father had any close relationship with David, but his Fresh Start came.

One major thing we need when our set time comes is an overflowing anointing.

"You prepare a table before me in the presence of my enemies. You anoint my head with oil; my (brimming) cup runs over." (Psalm 23:5)

"To everything there is a season, A time for every purpose under heaven." (Ecclesiastes 3:1)

There is time for a vision to be birth.

"(The Lord) said, I will surely return to you when the

season comes round, and behold, Sarah your wife will have a son. And Sarah was listening and heard it at the tent door which was behind Him." (Genesis 18:10 AMPC)

There is time for the process; there is time for the manifestation.

"The Lord visited Sarah as He had said, and the Lord did for her as He had promised. For Sarah became pregnant and bore Abraham a son in his old age, at the set time God had told him." (Genesis 21:1-2)

There is time for the completion.

"And the Lord answered me and said, Write the vision and engrave it so plainly upon tablets that everyone who passes may (be able to) read (it easily and quickly) as he hastens by. For the vision is yet for an appointed time and it hastens to the end (fulfillment); it will not deceive or disappoint. Though it tarry, wait (earnestly) for it, because it will surely come; it will not be behindhand on its appointed day." (Habakkuk 2:2-3)

You can activate the timing.

"Jesus said to her, (Dear) woman, what is that to you and to Me? (What do we have in common? Leave it to me.) My time (hour to act) has not yet come." (John 2:4)

There is time for everything on the earth; there is time for losses and for regaining. There is time for captivity and there is a time for freedom. There is time for suffering and there is time to enjoy.

God has set seasons, which come with their uniqueness, outlooks, demands, and grace. If you are not careful, sensitive, and observant you can miss your season of Fresh Start.

According to Dr Morris Cerullo, "The key to the spiritual breakthrough is timing." The key to Fresh Start is timing but we have to cease our opportunity. The woman with the issue of blood earlier mentioned (Mark 5:25) that she knew how important that moment was for her to ignore the crowd, paid no attention to the social discrimination against her. All she wanted was her restoration and she got it. She did not play with the time of her visitation at her disposal; she ignored the side talks and the pushers.

And (God) said to Abram, "Know positively that your descendants will be strangers dwelling as temporary residents in a land that is not theirs (Egypt), and they will be slaves there and will be afflicted and oppressed for 400 years." (Fulfilled in Exodus. 12:40.)

But I will bring judgment on that nation whom they will serve, and afterward they will come out with great possessions. (Acts 7:6, 7)

We need to activate the set time by taking definite steps.

We see how Daniel discovered the set time for the release of the children of Israel, he prayed to remind God and this led to their freedom.

"For thus says the Lord, When seventy years are completed for Babylon, I will visit you and keep My good promise to you, causing you to return to this place. For I know the thoughts and plans that I have for you, says the Lord, thoughts and plans for welfare and peace and not for evil, to give you hope in your final outcome.

Then you will call upon Me, and you will come and pray to Me, and I will hear and heed you. Then you will seek Me, inquire for, and require Me (as a vital necessity) and find Me when you search for Me with all your heart. I will be found by you, says the Lord, and I will release you from captivity and gather you from all the nations and all the places to which I have driven you, says the Lord, and I will bring you back to the place from which I caused you to be carried away captive." (Jeremiah 29:10-14 AMPC)

"In the first year of his reign, I, Daniel, understood from the books the number of years which, according to the word of the Lord to Jeremiah the prophet, must pass by before the desolations (which had been) pronounced on Jerusalem should end; and it was seventy years.

And I set my face to the Lord God to seek Him by prayer and supplications, with fasting and sackcloth and ashes; And I prayed to the Lord my God and made confession and said, O Lord, the great and dreadful God, Who keeps covenant, mercy, and loving-kindness with those who love Him and keep His commandments." (Daniel 9:2-4)

Suffering, Chastisement, or Reproach is not to be forever.

Comfort, comfort my people, says your God. Speak tenderly to the heart of Jerusalem, and cry to her that her time of service *and* her warfare are ended, that (her punishment is accepted and) her iniquity is pardoned, that she has received (punishment) from the Lord's hand double for all her sins. (Isaiah 40:1-2)

"And after you have suffered a little while, the God of all grace (Who imparts all blessing and favor), Who has called you to His (own) eternal glory in Christ Jesus, will Himself complete and make you what you ought to be, establish and ground you securely, and strengthen, and settle you." (1 Peter 5:10)

What is your responsibility?

Discern the time: When you cannot discern the time, you will miss a great deal in entering your Fresh Start.

A nation could not discern their season of Fresh Start.

"And they will dash you down to the ground, you (Jerusalem) and your children within you; and they will not leave in you one stone upon another, (all) because you did not come progressively to recognize and know and understand (from observation and experience) the time of your visitation (that is, when God was visiting you, the time in which God showed Himself gracious toward you and offered you salvation through Christ)." (Luke 19:44)

Be observant and sensitive.

Understand and appreciate the concept of time, to experience a Fresh Start and not miss it. You have to understand and appreciate the concept of time. The issue of time management

"(Even the migratory birds are punctual to their seasons.) Yes, the stork (excelling in the great height of her flight) in the heavens knows her appointed times (of migration), and the turtledove, the swallow, and the crane observe the time of their return. But My people do not know the law of the Lord (which the lower animals instinctively recognize in so far as it applies to them)." (Jeremiah 8:7)

Knowing what to do and do it at the right time, when you have a sense of time you will know what to do.

"And of Issachar, men who had understanding of the times to know what Israel ought to do, 200 chiefs; and all their kinsmen were under their command." (1 Chronicles 12:32)

The set time is a time for:

Mercy

He has (earnestly) remembered His mercy and loving-kindness, His truth and His faithfulness toward the house of Israel; all the ends of the earth have witnessed the salvation of our God. (Acts 13:47; 28:28.)

Remembrance

Do you feel neglected, unloved or abandoned? Do you think God has forgotten you? No! He has not forgotten. He is the invisible God that works behind the scenes to work the visible. For many years Jacob grieved not knowing that God was perfecting His work in his son. Joseph would have thought that the butler had forgotten him, but God orchestrated a situation of remembrance. May God remember you as He remembered Noah. It is your set time for remembrance in Jesus name.

When God remembered the Hebrews in the land of Egypt, bondage, struggles, afflictions, and oppression of 430 years was terminated and all wasted years and losses were paid back in one day. (Exodus 12:35-36) When God remembered Sarah, Rachel, Hannah, and Elizabeth reproach of barrenness gave way to fruitfulness. (Isaiah 49:15)

Reward and compensation

Do you think you have been denied a deserved promotion or compensation for any good you have done for others or even God's service? This is your season! Set time is when the Divinity decides to work with humanity to effect a change in situations. Call it a time of stepping out to step in; it produces manifestations of expectations and fulfilment. I join my faith with yours to declare boldly that it is your set time! (Hebrews 6:10; 11:6b; Acts 10:31; John 1:8; Isaiah 49:4; Nehemiah 5:19; 13:14; 1 Samuel 22:25

Revenge on the oppositions

(Proverbs 14:11; Luke 18:1-8; Judges 16:28; Psalms 18)

Recalling

(Genesis 40:14, 23; 41:9; 2 Samuel 9:1-12; Daniel 5:10-12; Esther 6:1-3)

Reproach removal

(Genesis 30:1-2; 22-24; Lamentations 5:1; Psalms 89:50; Isaiah 61:1; Luke 1:25; Genesis 18:9-15; 21:1-2)

Release and restoration

(Exodus 3:7-10,20;6:6;7:5;12;12:35-36; Isaiah 49:24-26;60 :1-22; 42:22)

Fresh Start Gem:"If you can't tolerate critics don't do anything new or interesting." - Jeff Bezos

❦

BE SENSITIVE AND RESPONSIVE
TO YOUR NEW SEASON

PRAYER POINTS

• Father, thank You for keeping me together with your love and truth. You are dependable and through God I can be exalted in Your strength; I will sing and praise your power. You are great, not quitting God!

• Father, arise and have mercy on me for my designated moment has come, forgive me and let warfare end in my life (Psalm 102:13; Isaiah 40:2; Romans 9:14-16; Luke 1:28,30)

• Father, grant me a visit that will terminate lingering problems, reward my waiting with... You are the rewarder of those that diligently seek You. Let there be manifestations of my due reward now, that Your glory may be revealed in my life, in the mighty name of Jesus (Luke 1:26; Isaiah 40:5; Genesis 21:1-7; Hebrews 6:11-15)

• Father, by Your intervention let everyone who needs to remember me for good begin to recall. Let me experience deliverance, and restoration where I need it (Numbers 13:14; Psalm 106:4; Jeremiah 15:15; Genesis 8:1)

• Father, grant me that kind of breakthrough that converts shame to glory, trial to testimony, failure to success, adversity to advancement, and disgrace to honor (1 Samuel 2:6-8; Joel 2:26-27; Isaiah 54:4; Romans 1:11-12)

ASSIGNMENT

• Write down the major lesson you've learned to unlock or activate your set time; Apply it.

DAY 8

QUALIFIED BY MERCY

PRAYER QUOTE:

"Prayer is the breath, the watchword, the comfort, the strength, the honor of a Christian." - Charles Spurgeon

SCRIPTURE:

"But this I recall and therefore have I hope and expectation: It is because of the Lord's mercy and loving-kindness that we are not consumed, because His [tender] compassions fail not. They are new every morning; great and abundant is Your stability and faithfulness." (Lamentations 3:21-23)

You are qualified for a FRESH START not because of any good you have done but because of God's mercy. neither should you imprison yourself to the prison of self condemnation, guilt and self judgement believing that you cannot have a FRESH START because of your past misdeed. Believe me if God should mark iniquities none of us we qualify for a FRESH START. God once told Moses, *"For I will show mercy to anyone I choose, and I will show compassion to anyone I choose."* (Exodus 33:19) and the same word was repeated in Romans 9:14-16:

"What shall we say then? Is there unrighteousness with God? Certainly not! For He says to Moses, "I will have mercy on whomever I will have mercy, and I will have compassion on whomever I will have compassion." So then it is not of him who wills, nor of him who runs, but of God who shows mercy."

Mercy is God's gift and it has to be received when it is extended. What is this "Mercy" being talked about? In the simplest definition, mercy is compassion or forgiveness shown toward someone whom it is within one's power to punish or harm." Some of the synonyms are: leniency, compassion, grace, pity, forgiveness, kindness, tolerance, indulgence, magnanimity, sympathy, forbearance.

A person who, for instance, has gotten abortions in the past may feel they don't deserve to have children and be under self-condemnation, but God is a God of many second chances. Mercy will qualify you where your past disqualifies. In recent times many have retorted that the marriage of Megan Markle to Prince Harry is an act of mercy considering all odds against her.

What God's mercy will do for you is to empower you for your FRESH START; so you don't continue to play victim to your past mistakes.

"In Whom we have our redemption through His blood, [which means] the forgiveness of our sins." (Colossians 1:14)

"If we confess our sins, he is faithful and just to forgive us our sins, and to cleanse us from all unrighteousness." (1 John 1:9)

I have had many Fresh Starts. One of those Fresh Starts, I was in a rut I caused by my stupidity and negligence. For over seven years I was here, and even when God was ready to let me out, I was so scared to come out. I was full of shame, with my head bowed with guilt, but I heard God speak, "There is, therefore now no condemnation... (Romans 8:1-2) Praise God for His mercies!

Do you remember the woman caught in adultery and the woman with the beautiful alabaster (John 8:1-11; Luke 7:36-50) Indeed, God will have mercy on whom He will have mercy, but the one to whom it is extended must be able to receive it. (Romans 9:14-16)

One person in history that best captured this concept was a man who was blind, but desperate enough to tap into the mercy of God through Jesus. His story could be found in the book of Marks chapter 10 and verses 46-52. He did not appeal to Jesus by referencing to his pedigree or degree, experience, or exposure, but by the mercies of God as a qualification for his proposed change of situation and that was what got Jesus to help him.

For acceptance and maximization of the abundant mercies of God you will need to:

- **Create a System:** Choose to depend on God rather than your ability or looking down at yourself but looking up to Jesus (Proverbs 3:5-6; Hebrews 12:1-2)

- **Close Gaps:** Gaps drains effort, reduces values, and contaminates or affects the result of a life or project. identify self -created or induced gaps and ensure you close such, "For the scepter of wickedness shall not rest on the land allotted to the righteous, lest the righteous reach out their hands in iniquity." (Psalm 125:3) Most often you will hear telling the people that got their FRESH START from Him, "Go and sin no more." Simply saying stop whatever set you backward before.

- **Identify Distractions:** In the world that we are today, distractions are everywhere. Most distractions may not appear as people or things that are bad, but seemingly good things. Also people that will always want you to compromise God's standard and the personal decisions you have made. Hence, they are major distractors from focus. So, we must identify them and learn to do away with them by self-discipline.

• **Shed the Weight:** Some cups will never pass over us, but we must drink them. They are the pathways to a FRESH START. You must be able to subject yourself to go through the required refining process for you to have your FRESH START. Apart from appealing to the mercy of God, the blind Bartimaeus ignored the mockers. To obtain your FRESH START, one thing you have to do is ignore both the mocker, the critics and even the cheerleaders. Also, temptations to compromise on God's standards might come our way but we must be able to say, "Lord not as I will, but as you will." Waiting can be tempting and in the course of waiting many will suggest alternatives but stay on!

• **Identify time Wasters:** Time waster may be people or unnecessary things that we may have given more attention to than they really deserve.

• **Eliminate time Wasters:** Time wasters must not just be identified but eliminated. We eliminate time wasters by consciously focusing on who and what are necessary at every moment.

• **Be Accountable:** Accountability is a very good virtue a person can possess. It will help one to track his or her progress and take appropriate decisions where necessary. Your coach or mentor could be your accountability partner.

- **Celebrate Milestones:** You may not have arrived at the desired destination yet but count your blessings, give yourself some part on the back for how far. Count your blessings as you move along. In life's journey, we must learn to acknowledge the hand of God to give thanks to God for the victory in every moment of life. Victory in significant events should not be considered unnecessary but should be celebrated.

- **Don't Give Up:** No matter your mistakes, no matter your past, don't give up on yourself for God has not given up on you!

Fresh Start Gem: "Every moment is a fresh beginning."
- T. S. Eliot

✤
MERCY IS THE QUALIFYING FACTOR

PRAYER POINTS

- I worship You, EL RACHUM, the merciful God. I'm sure You will not forsake me, neither destroy me, nor forget Your covenant of mercy. I am grateful for Your mercies towards me over the years. (Deuteronomy 4:31; Lamentations 3:21-22)

- Father, I receive divine enablement to embrace, walk, and express your mercies every day in Jesus name (Lamentations 3:22-23; Psalm 89:1)

- Father, let Your mercy terminate every accusation, judgment, condemnation (self or imposed) speaking and standing against my Fresh Start, breakthroughs, blessings and next level. I rebuke every opposing force against the manifestation of God's glory and power in my life in the name of Jesus (Joshua 3:1-3; Isaiah 54:17; Mark 10:56-52)

• Father, let Your mercy locate me in this season, convert my story to glory, my shame to honor in the mighty name of Jesus (Psalm 126)

• Father, let Your goodness and mercy be my companion all the days of my life. Let mercy speak for me where I cannot defend myself, let the blood of Jesus speak mercy on my behalf (Psalm 23:6; Hebrew 12:24)

ASSIGNMENT

• Have a critical evaluation of your life and prayerfully make a list of areas where you need to embrace the mercies of God for victorious living.

DAY 9

GIVE ME THIS
MOUNTAIN

PRAYER QUOTE:

"Our prayers lay the track down on which God's power can come. Like a mighty locomotive, his power is irresistible, but it cannot reach us without rails." - Watchman Nee

"Then the children of Judah came to Joshua in Gilgal. And Caleb the son of Jephunneh the Kenizzite said to him: "You know the word which the Lord said to Moses the man of God concerning you and me in Kadesh Barnea. I was forty years old when Moses the servant of the Lord sent me from Kadesh Barnea to spy out the land, and I brought back word to him as it was in my

heart. Nevertheless my brethren who went up with me made the heart of the people melt, but I wholly followed the Lord my God. So Moses swore on that day, saying, 'Surely the land where your foot has trodden shall be your inheritance and your children's forever, because you have wholly followed the Lord my God.' And now, behold, the Lord has kept me alive, as He said, these forty-five years, ever since the Lord spoke this word to Moses while Israel wandered in the wilderness; and now, here I am this day, eighty-five years old. As yet I am as strong this day as on the day that Moses sent me; just as my strength was then, so now is my strength for war, both for going out and for coming in. Now therefore, give me this mountain of which the Lord spoke in that day; for you heard in that day how the Anakim were there, and that the cities were great and fortified. It may be that the Lord will be with me, and I shall be able to drive them out as the Lord said." And Joshua blessed him, and gave Hebron to Caleb the son of Jephunneh as an inheritance. Hebron therefore became the inheritance of Caleb the son of Jephunneh the Kenizzite to this day, because he'd wholly followed the Lord God of Israel. And the name of Hebron formerly was Kiryat Arba (Arba was the greatest man among the Anakim). Then the land had rest from war." (Joshua 14:6-15)

For your Fresh Start, you must lay claim to and insist on every word the Lord has spoken concerning you to see it come to reality in your life.

"Mountain" could mean so many things, including:

The mountain in this context signifies a promise and

an inheritance somewhere that he (Caleb) believed God for, he held on to it for 40 years.

For some, the mountain may represent an overwhelming challenge, which is fierce. The cry of Caleb reflects a desperate man who it desires to experience victory, just as the case of the blind man in Luke 18:35-42 who desperately desired a change in His predicament. Fresh Start is a journey into a whole new experience of marital bliss, of a thriving business, financial abundance, or whatsoever promise you may have received from God.

When we know God's precious promises for our lives and are convinced of them, it instills boldness to insist until we lay hold of them. Give me this mountain signifies the voice of a man who refuses to take no for an answer, saying I know this is mine. This is what God has destined for me or destined me for, it's a voice of someone that knows where they are going, saying, this is mine and I cannot let it go. It's the earnest claim of a long-term promise of God based on His integrity.

The bible says *"God is not a man, that He should lie, nor a son of man, that He should repent. Has He said, and will He not do? Or has He spoken, and will He not make it good?"* (Numbers 23:19)

It does not matter your age, gender, or your experience in life. That which God has promised you, will eventually manifest if you persistently lay hold on His word and pray through.

The story revealed the kind of person Caleb was

and I believe one can learn from him. Caleb was a "possibility thinker," one who sees himself walking into the future, not alone, but leaning on the strong arm of his God; he followed the Lord wholly. Please pause to ask yourself, Am I following God fully right now? Am I fully obedient? What in me needs to change so I can align myself with God? Be your critic but don't be under condemnation

What is required for you to possess the mountain?

1. **Connection:** There is no substitute for fellowship with the Holy Spirit in your Fresh Start journey. There would always be contentions against whatever God has promised you. There would be people and powers that would want to stand in your way, so you need to be connected to God. Caleb's pursuit was not something he wanted, but what God promised him through Moses. The bible recorded that he followed the Lord wholly, he was conscious of God's presence and its benefits. Secondly, you need to connect to people. There are people to your FRESH START just like Naomi was to Ruth, The Butler to Joseph (Genesis 40:14;41:9-14)

2. **Right attitude:** To possess your mountain, you must be ready not to take a NO for an answer, just like Caleb and the woman with the issue of blood (in Mark 5:25-29). She desired a Fresh Start and she went for it. The Syrophoenician woman who came to Jesus was not dismayed by the words He said but was resilient getting healing for her

daughter. (Mathew 15:22-29) If you believe in God for a Fresh Start for you or someone in your household, such a person can receive it because of your relentless faith. You can turn your pain to gain or You can decide to let it have you or you have it. You can call it Determination!

3. **Faith:** We call Abraham "father", not because he got God's attention by living like a saint, but because God made something out of Abraham when he was a nobody. Isn't that what we've always read in Scripture, God saying to Abraham, "I set you up as the father of many peoples"? Abraham was first named "father" and then became a father because he dared to trust God to do what only God could do: raise the dead to life, with a word, make something out of nothing. When everything was hopeless, Abraham believed anyway, deciding not to live by what he saw he couldn't do, but on what God said he would do. And so he was made the father of a multitude of peoples. God himself said to him, "You're going to have a big family, Abraham!" Abraham didn't focus on his own impotence and say, "It's hopeless. This hundred-year-old body could never father a child." Nor did he survey Sarah's decades of infertility and give up. The bible says he (Abraham) staggered not at the promises of God through unbelief but was strong in faith. (Rom 4: 20). The same applies to us; those who do not stagger at the promises of God through unbelief will stand strong (in faith) to experience the reality of God's word.

And Jesus, replying, said to them, Have faith in God [constantly]. (Mark 11:22)

Everyone who obtained the promises of God for their lives obtained it through faith and patience.

4. **Patience:** The Bible admonishes us to *"imitate those who through faith and patience inherit the promises".* (Hebrews 6:12)

"Blessed (happy, to be envied) is the man who is patient under trial and stands up under temptation, for when he has stood the test and been approved, he will receive [the victor's] crown of life which God has promised to those who love Him. (James 1:12)

It doesn't just take faith alone to obtain the promises of God for us, but faith and patience. Between the time you received a word from God -for any area of your life- and the time it manifests there must be an exercise of patience. When we are not patient, we compromise and miss God's best for our lives.

5. **Persistence:** To really obtain God's best for our lives, we must be persistent. Persistence also means steadfastness- to stand steady even in the face of restrictions and challenges. The oppositions should strengthen you and not stop you. Persistent people never take no for an answer, they never give up at the first trial, they continue until they win. They say yes to challenges; You have to give on up, I'm not ready to quit; Mountain get out of my way because I must pass through. Jacob wrestled with

the Lord (see Gen 32: 22-32) and his words were that of a persistent person. It requires diligence to be persistent.

Now when He saw that He did not prevail against him, He touched the socket of his hip; and the socket of Jacob's hip was out of joint as He wrestled with him. And He said, "Let Me go, for the day breaks. "But he said, "I will not let You go unless You bless me!" (Genesis 32:25-26)

You are not to settle for failure because you are not a failure; you are to wrestle until you prevail by laying hold on the promises of God until it becomes an experience.

6. **Commitment:** Caleb followed the LORD "wholeheartedly", with complete fidelity. What a testimony! So often many follow the Lord with a partially committed heart, or when it suits them. To fully experience and enjoy God's best for us; we must lean on faith rather than sight with total commitment to our role. Fear sets in, and we follow our fears instead of our faith. To be committed to a cause requires discipline!

Also, we have to be conscious of the fact that our Fresh Start is not something we can do by ourselves; for a mountain to remove, it will take a force of faith. So, stop trying to figure it out yourself. Employ the force of the supernatural in God.

"What then shall we say to these things? If God is for us, who can be against us? He who did not spare His own

Son, but delivered Him up for us all, how shall He not with Him also freely give us all things?" (Romans 8:31-33)

Irrespective of whatsoever is standing in your way they shall become plain, they shall not be seen anymore. For this is the word of the Lord to you.

I can tell you this fact, a FRESH START is not going to be given on a platter of gold, and you have to work it out, but you will succeed with the help of God! (Psalm 121)

Fresh Start Gem: "Life is ten percent what happens to you and ninety percent how you react to it." - John C. Maxwell

❧

STAND FIRM: CLAIM WHAT IS DULY YOURS

PRAYER POINTS

• I worship You Jehovah EL MUNAH, the faithful God, who keeps covenant for a thousand generations, is anything too hard for you the God of all flesh. Father, release fresh strength and grace to overcome every opposition and the stubborn situation in my life. I reject every evil demand upon my life in Jesus Name! (Deuteronomy 7:9; Jeremiah 32:27)

• Father, just as Caleb had a different spirit to pursue the seemingly impossible, release strength to my inner man that empowers me to stand against every resisting force in this season of a Fresh Start. (Isaiah 41:10-14)

• I come against ungodly diversion, denial, deflection, detour, or delay manifestations of my Fresh Start

• Now is the time for manifestation. I receive the strength to bring forth. Now Lord, reveal your glory and power upon me and through me by notable miracles and breakthroughs (Isaiah 37:3)

• Father, let the wickedness of the wicked against my Fresh Start come to an end. I command the wicked to be uprooted from what is rightfully mine. O Lord let the wasters and destroyers be far away from me.

ASSIGNMENTS

• Identify the present challenge you are faced with and ask God to show you the way out of it.

• Write out (through meditation) and in detail the steps you have to take to overcome such challenges.

• Take action!

DAY 10

TAPPING INTO THE STRENGTH OF GOD

PRAYER QUOTE:

"We can change the course of event, if we go to our knees in believing prayer." - Evangelist Billy Graham

SCRIPTURE:

"Even the youths shall faint and be weary, and the young men shall utterly fall: But they that wait upon the Lord shall renew their strength; they shall mount up with wings as eagles; they shall run, and not be weary; and they shall walk, and not faint." (Isaiah 40:30-31)

The journey of Fresh Start, I will not deceive you, is not going to be an easy thing, it is a process and there are days you become tired and weary because you cannot see that desired change in sight or the things you see and hear. That is why you need that external boost. That was why Nehemiah declared, the joy of the Lord is your strength (Nehemiah 8:10)

As you must have learned from day 8, you have to embrace the mercies of God in securing your Fresh Start. So you also have to know how to maximize the strength to handle the stress without (1 John 4:4) Don't be pressed down by the external weights, they are devil's means of discouraging you from the pursuit of your Fresh Start.

"Now unto him that is able to do exceeding abundantly above all that we ask or think, according to the power that worketh in us." (Ephesians .3:20)

There is a power at work in You! But you have to activate it.

"...It is enough; now, O LORD, take away my life; for I am not better than my fathers." (1 Kings 19:4c)

The above statement came from a mighty prophet, Elijah. It was an expression of deep sorrow and depression as a result of his present challenges. Although he had been used mightily by God to destroy the prophets of Baal, shut heaven from raining, and later praying for it to rain, Elijah's strength failed him at this point and he was almost giving up. But God's strength was available for him. He was fed with the angel food.

"And as he lay and slept under a juniper tree, behold, then an angel touched him, and said unto him, arise and eat. And he looked, and, behold, there was a cake baken on the coals, and a cruse of water at his head. And he did eat and drink, and laid him down again. And the angel of the Lord came the second time again, and touched him, and said, Arise and eat; because the journey is too great for thee. And he arose, and did eat and drink, and went in the strength of that meat forty days and forty nights unto Horeb the mount of God." [1 Kings 19:5-8]

At his lowest moment, God showed up for Elijah and strengthened him. This might also be a low moment for you. It may appear like all hope is lost and that human effort has failed. Beloved, rest assured that God never fails and that you can tap into His strength to keep you going.

How Do You Tap Into God's Strength?

First, you must come to the end of yourself. That is, you must totally surrender your situation to the Lord. After Simon Peter and his friends had worked all night in the sea without catching a single fish, they were very discouraged and helpless. Just in time, Jesus showed up ashore and requested that they lend him their boat. At the end of His address, Jesus instructed that the fishermen throw in their net once again into the sea for a catch. It is worthy of note that these experienced fishermen had used all known strategies throughout the night without success. They must have been very surprised at the words of Jesus, but they obeyed and got their biggest miracle. (Luke 5:1-7)

The Strength that God provides come from the Holy Spirit and that strength is available in every situation (John 14:16, 26)

Secondly, to tap into God's strength you must be ready to follow His lead. Jesus said, "My sheep hear my voice, and I know them, and they follow me." [John 10:27] Walking with God is a conscious effort, to listen and act on His instructions. When you are led by the Spirit of God, you can never come into error. This is why you need His strength. There will be times when all human calculations and estimations fail, God cannot fail. He is all wise and all-knowing, a present help in time of need. God's strength is His grace in our life. When Apostle Paul prayed that the thorn in his flesh is taken away, Jesus told him that His grace is sufficient for him.

"And lest I should be exalted above measure through the abundance of the revelations, there was given to me a thorn in the flesh, the messenger of Satan to buffet me, lest I should be exalted above measure. For this thing I besought the Lord thrice, that it might depart from me. And he said unto me, My grace is sufficient for thee: for my strength is made perfect in weakness. Most gladly therefore will I rather glory in my infirmities, that the power of Christ may rest upon me." (2 Corinthians 12:7-9)

When we engage the grace of God we engage His strength. In the journey to a Fresh Start you have to tap into God's strength. So today, tap into that strength. Honestly, some days will be harder than the rest, but those are the days that I sing songs like, "You are my strength" by William Murphy

"Trust in the Lord with all your heart; and lean not on your own understanding. In all your ways acknowledge Him and He will direct your path." (Proverbs 3:5-6)

There are also situations beyond your human ability, but you can draw strength from God to overcome. We see an example when David, a young teenage boy, went all out to fight a professional warrior, Goliath of Gath. (See 1 Samuel 17). David won the battle, not because he was so skilled in the art of war, nor because he had so much ammunition or weapons of war, but because he trusted the God of Israel to grant him victory over the uncircumcised Philistine. (1 Samuel 17:45-47)

David was so confident about His God, that he never allowed himself to be frightened by the height of Goliath. Of course, he knew that his God is bigger than any human soldier. This should also be your mindset on this journey of Fresh Start as you face oppositions and challenges to your Fresh Start, which I can assure you will overcome.

No situation is too difficult for God to bring a solution to, rest in His unfailing strength today. Your confidence increases when you study His word and put it to practice. Scriptures say those who know their God shall be strong and they shall do exploits. (Daniel 11:32b). And let this be your confession always: *"I can do all things through Christ who strengthens me."* (Philippians 4:13)

Fresh Start Gem: "We gain strength, and courage, and confidence by each experience in which we really stop to look fear in the face… we must do that which think we cannot." - Eleanor Roosevelt

✤

THERE IS NOTHING YOU CANNOT DO!

PRAYER POINTS

• Heavenly Father, I am grateful for Your strength that is always available for me in times of need. I declare, You are MY STRENGTH! I am grateful for your timely and timeless help (Psalm 28:7;46)

• Father, help me to walk supernatural in divine strength from now on, out of Your glorious riches please strengthen me with power through Your Spirit in my inner being. Let my strength equal my days, I have the joy that produces strength and that strength is being renewed continually. My frame is receiving strength. I am like a well-watered garden in Jesus' name. (Ephesians 3:16; Deuteronomy 33:25;2 Chronicles 16:9; Nehemiah 8:10; Isaiah 40:31; 58:11)

• Father, I receive victory over every persistent challenge in my life. I receive strength for my faith,

I come against doubt and unbelief in Jesus name (Psalm 84:5-7 Romans 4:20)

• I exercise my authority in Christ and I decree that I will never be afraid or frightened by the opposition in Jesus name.

• I prophesy that divine wisdom is made available to me in this journey, in every area, in Jesus' name

• I receive divine strength in my physical body and I say NO to sickness and disease in Jesus' name.

ASSIGNMENT

• List out areas where you need the strength of God and prayerfully apply His strength to each.

DAY 11

❧

UNLEASHING THE POWER IN THE WORD

PRAYER QUOTE:

"Pray like you have never prayed before. Pray like you were dying, like it's your last minute." - William Branham

SCRIPTURE:

"In the beginning God created the heavens and the earth. The earth was without form, and void; and darkness was on the face of the deep. And the Spirit of God was hovering over the face of the waters. Then God said, "Let there be light"; and there was light. 4 And God saw the light that it was good; and God divided the light from the darkness." (Genesis 1:1-5)

Your Fresh Start starts with the Word of God, written or spoken. For instance, I reliably picked it up in the Spirit about this journey and the written Word to back it up. This is the same Word that launched Peter into his Fresh Start journey when Jesus spoke to him to launch out into the deep after laboring without anything to show for it. (Luke 5:1-10) It was the Word that Mary also heard that launched her into the realm of possibilities despite the impossibilities surrounding her. (Luke 1:26 -38)

We see that in the beginning, the word of God created the heaven and the earth. We can see from the text that no situation or challenge is unchangeable or impossible for God. If the word of God could create the heaven and earth, how difficult are your present circumstances that it cannot be figured out by God's word. The centurion soldier in the Bible realized the power of the word of God and he said to Jesus *"… but speak the word, and my servant shall be healed"* (Matthew 8:8)

The Bible says "Thou (God) hast magnified thy word above all thy name (Psalms 138:2). This shows to us that God will never allow His word to fall to the ground. He is active and alert watching over his word to perform it. (Jeremiah 1:12b)

It is God's nature to call forth the things that are not as though they were and as children of God, we must learn to think God's thoughts, speak God's word, and do God's word. The father's word in lips ruled by faith will be like His word in Jesus's lips.

For a Fresh Start, you must learn to confess the Word of God because words are seeds sown into the future. Therefore, you must learn to sow good seeds. Regardless of your present circumstances, the Lord has declared to us, we are more than a conqueror hallelujah! So, declare that I am blessed, my marriage is blessed; my business is blessed; my children are blessed; I am destined to be above and not beneath; failure is defeated; poverty is defeated; dangerous habits are broken; barrenness is broken. Whatever the situation is, it is turned to good in Jesus name.

Apart from the fact that the word of God is creative in nature, the word of God can also heal. It is clear from the record of the scriptures that sicknesses and diseases whatsoever cannot withstand the power of the spoken word of God. (Psalm 107:20) In Luke 5:17, Jesus was teaching, and the power of God was present to heal. This explains to us that, as He was teaching, the Word was stirring the power and the power went into operation to bring about their healing. Therefore, God's Word is the stirrer up of power. A man once said that "the power within lies dormant until the Word stirs it into operation."

Also, in the scriptures, we read Matthew 8:16 that many were *"brought unto Jesus who were possessed with devils: and he cast out the spirits **with his word** and healed all that were sick."*

"This Book of the Law shall not depart from your mouth, but you shall meditate in it day and night, that you may observe to do according to all that is written in it. For then you will make your way prosperous, and then you will have good success." (Joshua 1:8)

This scripture reveals that we can make our way prosperous and have good success with the instrument of the word.

"For then you will make your way prosperous, and then you will have good success." (Joshua 1:8)

Our success is determined by us and not by the devil. Hallelujah!

For God's word to produce the desired results in and through you, you must receive it, believe it, act on it, and make it your confessions.

- Receive the word

Word of God discovered and applied compels the Spirits of God at work in you to act. If you need counsel, go to the Word, study it, meditate on it. When we listen to or study the word of God with an open heart, the Spirit of Counsel tells you what next step to take.

The Holy Spirit is called our teacher. When the Holy Spirit – the Spirit of Revelation - teaches you on any subject, this is called an encounter with depths of His Word.

Every operation of the Holy Spirit is traceable to the discovery made in the Word of God. In this season of a Fresh Start, you need to gain deeper access into the Word for greater exploits. No one can ever have a greater experience than his depth in the Word. It is the Word that provokes the power of God unto salvation to everyone that believes (Romans 1:16).

- Believe the word

Once the Word gains entrance into the heart of a man, he has compelled the manifestation of signs and wonders. He may not need to pray, but the moment he encounters the Word of God on any subject, he has switched on the miraculous. Think of Abraham. (Romans 4:18-24)

It is the Word of God that makes you a commander of signs. Therefore, no accomplishment is authentic; no miracle is genuine, until it is founded upon the Word.

- Do the word

"But be doers of the word, and not hearers only, deceiving yourselves. 23 For if anyone is a hearer of the word and not a doer, he is like a man observing his natural face in a mirror; 24 for he observes himself, goes away, and immediately forgets what kind of man he was. 25 But he who looks into the perfect law of liberty and continues in it, and is not a forgetful hearer but a doer of the work, this one will be blessed in what he does." (James 1:22-25 NKJV)

It is clear from the scriptures that it is the doers of the word of God that shall be blessed in what they do. God's integrity is committed to delivering what the word of God says when we live by the word. So, we search the mind of God for every area of our lives and partner with the Holy spirit in acting on it respectively with all confidence.

- Confess the word

"Death and Life are in the power of the tongue..." (Proverbs 18:21)

In every challenging situation of life, put your mouth to work because there is power in the tongue. God has not destined you to fail. Never! His thoughts toward you are thoughts of peace and not of evil to give you a future and a hope. (Jeremiah 29:11)

So, never conclude on what God has not concluded on.

Who told you your marriage will not work, who told you that sickness or disease will not bow, who told you that business will not survive or become great, who told you?

That marriage will work! Sickness or diseases will bow! That business will thrive! Those children will succeed! That habit will be broken! As you say it, you see it, in Jesus Name.

Moses spoke before Pharaoh until they-the people of Israel- finally left Egypt. He kept saying, *"Let my people go"*. These were not his words but the word of God.

"You shall also decide and decree a thing, and it shall be established for you; and the light [of God's favor] shall shine upon your ways." (Job 22:28 AMP)

You don't stop speaking until what you want is affected.

Fresh Start Gem: "Battles are fought in our minds every day. When we begin to feel the battle is just too difficult and want to give up, we must choose to resist negative thoughts and be determined to rise above our problems. We must decide that we're not going to quit. When we're bombarded with doubts and fears, we must take a stand and say: 'I'll never give up! God's on my side. He loves me, and He's helping me! I'm going to make it!" - **Joyce Meyer**

"You are not only responsible for what you say, but also for what you do not say." Martin Luther

❁

STAND UPON THE WORD
NO MATTER WHAT

PRAYER POINTS

- I declare that my mind is sound, and my heart is receptive to the word of God as I commit myself to study the word of God (Psalm 119:33-40)

• Father, empower me to do the seemingly impossible, to accomplish long time dreams and to receive due and overdue promises. I pull down every image, argument, theory, and reasoning of impossibility (1 Corinthians 10:4-5)

• Father, help me from this day that I may begin to see myself the way you see me (Psalm 139;Judges 6:12;11:1)

• I come against stronghold limiting me. By God's grace, I shall complete my tasks, projects, and assignments. Not only that I'm empowered to successfully complete my assignment, but God's presence is with me and I'm ready and up to the task ahead and failure is not an option! (Isaiah 40:1-2;)

• Father, in this new season of a Fresh Start, do exceedingly great things around me that provokes new songs (2 Samuel 2: 1-10)

ASSIGNMENT

• Search for the word of God in the scriptures that address your challenges, meditate on them, and open your heart to believe them.

• What are you telling yourself? Reject the negative thoughts coming to your mind about your Fresh Start.

• Commit yourself to confessing the word of God and make a decision to never speak what God has not said concerning you. Today, start speaking positive things; it is possible, I can have it, I can become it, I can do it.

DAY 12

NO MORE RESTRICTIONS

PRAYER QUOTE:

"None can believe how powerful prayer and what it is able to affect but those who have learned it by experience." - Martin Luther

SCRIPTURE:

"God's Message to his anointed, to Cyrus, whom he took by the hand. To give the task of taming the nations, of terrifying their kings—He gave him free rein, no restrictions: "I'll go ahead of you, clearing and paving the road. I'll break down bronze city gates, smash padlocks, kick down barred entrances. I'll lead you to buried

treasures, secret caches of valuables—Confirmations that it is, in fact, I, God, the God of Israel, who calls you by your name. It's because of my dear servant Jacob, Israel my chosen, That I've singled you out, called you by name, and given you this privileged work. And you don't even know me! I am God, the only God there is. Besides me there are no real gods. I'm the one who armed you for this work, though you don't even know me, So that everyone, from east to west, will know that I have no god-rivals. I am God, the only God there is. I form light and create darkness, I make harmonies and create discords. I, God, do all these things." (Isaiah 45:1-7)

WHAT ARE RESTRICTIONS?

Restrictions are limiting factors that keep one in a certain boundary and hinder one from moving forward. They are the barriers between where you are and where you ought to be. In fact, they keep people from achieving God's best for their life. Restrictions are limiting conditions or measure which could be legal or illegal. It could be visible or invisible to you and the only way you can know are by the signs and symptoms generated by their presence.

WHY RESTRICTIONS

- To stop you from achieving your goals of fulfilling your divine purpose and plans

- To confine you in a certain adverse or negative situation

- To stop you from moving forward

- To stop you from attaining a greater height

WHAT ARE THE RESTRICTIONS

1. WALLS. Walls create barriers between you and your helpers, the indication of that is the unwillingness of helpers to help you or sudden withdrawal of helpers from continuing to help you. Walls also create artificial or temporary immobility. It was recorded in the book of Joshua 1 and verse 7, "Jericho was shut up tight as a drum because of the people of Israel: no one going in, and no one coming out." Just like saying, nobody is making any offers to you, so you will not make any offers to anybody. Walls are erected in the spirit realm to limit a person. It is invisible and spiritual. It could affect and limit you socially, physically, maritally, financially, emotionally, or spiritually. Walls hold people in bondage.

2. GATES. Gates are meant for protection providing security for the people within but spiritually serves negatively as means of barrier placed on the life of a person to hinder movement upward or forward (Psalm 24:7-10) If gates are not dealt with hinder flows of blessings and favors from coming in. When a man called by King Cyrus was called to go on assignment for God, God promised him, "I will go before you and break and make the crooked places straight; I will break in pieces the gates of bronze and cut the bars of iron." (Isaiah 45:3) Gates in the biblical times also meant elders, that is decision makers which in modern times mean men of influence, decision makers, executives, and

lawmakers; men and women in power who make or influence decisions that could affect your FRESH START negatively or positively. They are part of environmental threats or opportunities to your FRESH START. (Ruth 4:11; Deuteronomy 16:18).

Gate could also mean entry point, or a stronghold imprisoning our thought and belief system (2 Corinthians 10:4-5). Our five senses are gateways into our lives, causing emotional or mental blockages; our distorted thought patterns, doubts, unbelief, fear, negativity, reasonings, if you don't deal with them it could create blockage to achieving your goals (Proverbs 4:11) It does not matter the presence of 'gates' you will complete your project, you will accomplish your goals. Gates cannot hold you back forever. Every gate of impudence, effrontery, and resistance shall crumble.

3. ROADBLOCKS. They're meant to spiritually hold a person back from entering and maximizing a divine purpose (1 Samuel 23:7) Imagine embarking on a journey all made for your traveling, navigation figured out and suddenly you get to a point and you meet the sign, "Road closed"? Your immediate reaction is anger, then you quickly think of the next route option. God helps you so that your navigation system is okay. Physical roadblocks or spiritual roadblocks cause delay, detour, and discouragement. Sometimes roadblocks are means used to make a pause to avoid any destruction along the pathway of our

journey in destiny. When you come to that halt, pause and ponder; is it God or the Devil?

4. MOUNTAINS. In the spiritual context mountains represent major barriers, which could become an obstacle to achieving a set goal or accomplishing a project. Challenges in relative to your FRESH START may also be described as mountains. And it could be financial, physical, emotional, relational, or in the form of personnel. When God asked Zerubbabel to embark on the building project for Him, he was forewarned about the "mountain ahead of him, but at the same time the solution was already planned, to For who are you, O great mountain [of human obstacles]? Before Zerubbabel [who with Joshua had led the return of the exiles from Babylon and was undertaking the rebuilding of the temple, before him] you shall become a plain [a mere]molehill]! And he shall bring forth the finishing gable stone [of the new temple] with loud shoutings of the people, crying, Grace, grace to it! (Zechariah 4:7) You have the power and the grace to look at your "mountain" to move and it will move. (Psalm 46:2; Mark 11:22; Psalm 97:5; Psalm 114:4; Isaiah 64:4)

5. OTHER STUFF. Like earlier mentioned, restrictions are stoppers and limiting factors. What are the other things that could stop or limit you? Sudden sickness, sudden distress: financial, emotional, or mental. Threats, demonic oppositions, to know how oppositions are used to

stop people from the pursuit of FRESH -START, study the book of Nehemiah. You should however know and have the assurance, "What, then shall we say in response to these things? If God is for us, who can be against us?" (Romans 8:31) You cannot ignore human obstacles which come in the forms of - fault-finders, accusers, haters, and distractors.

Consider the verse 2 of our text carefully: *I will go before you and will level the mountains; I will break down gates of bronze and cut through bars of iron.*

Mountains are simply restrictions, challenges, or even principalities, and God is giving us His word that He is going to take care of them. *For this reason, he sent his son to destroy the works of the devil* (I John 3:8) even if they are powers or principalities that might have restricted you, you can rest assured that you are entering a new era in Jesus name. Allow this to settle within you; restrictions are not meant to last forever; they are meant to be overcome.

"The suffering won't last forever. It won't be long before this generous God who has great plans for us in Christ— eternal and glorious plans they are!—will have you put together and on your feet for good. He gets the last word; yes, he does." (1 Peter 5:810-11)

You and God are the Ultimate Determinant of Your Fresh Start; trying to fix it your way can complicate issues for you and others in the long run.

Delay is not denial. God has a plan for the delay.

Don't give up on the goal of a FRESH START just because of the fierceness of challenges. Delay is not denial!

Have you given up on the word of the Lord spoken to you because of the past setbacks or present challenges? Know this, God is bigger than your challenges! Go back to your journal, what is your area of expectations? What are your desires? What actions are expected on your side?

God is moving you forward and nothing can stop you, nothing can hinder your progress. You cannot allow Satan to restrict you nor hinder you from your Fresh Start. That is the word of God saying no more restrictions or barriers. Nothing that has restricted you this far can restrict you further in Jesus name.

Fresh Start Gem: "Once we accept our limits, we go beyond them." - Albert Einstein

✤

YOU CAN OVERCOME THAT OBSTACLE!

PRAYER POINTS

• Father, I praise You as the mountain mover and with Your presence, there is no mountain that cannot be moved. Move mightily in my life in this season, begin to oppose, and destroy any power masquerading behind any misfortune in my life, for this reason you sent your son to destroy the works of darkness (1 John 3:8; Isaiah 64:1-5)

• I command every mountain of impossibility before me to become plain in the mighty name of Jesus. All things are working in my favor and to my advantage. All obstacles are turning to stepping stones. I command every contrary image, imagination, that is contrary to the promise of God for my FRESH START to be consumed by fire in the mighty name of Jesus. I come against the operations and activities of the spirit of fear, timidity, inadequacy, and instead I receive boldness, courage, (Joshua 1:19] (Zechariah 4:7; Isaiah 41:15;)

• I refuse to stay in the valley of stagnation, frustration, and rejection. Everything that stands as a limitation in my way, I pull you down in Jesus name. I'm delivered from any form distress that could stop me- mental, emotional, physical, spiritual, financial or social. I boldly declare, I shall not lack any good thing beneficial to my FRESH START. I'm breaking through all restrictions, I'm moving forward and upward. I command every satanic opposition and confrontation to crumble (Psalm 34; Isaiah 40:4; 2 Samuel 5:20)

• Father, perfect all that concerns my health and wellbeing – emotional, physical, mental, financial, and spiritual. I command you the spirit of infirmity to lose your hold upon my life. I claim and receive total healing in all areas of my life. I receive the touch of God for total healings and restoration.

• Father, empower my hands to finish that which you have started through me and anoint me to receive that which you have started for me in Jesus name, my project and dreams shall not become an abandoned project. I declare my projects and programs shall not lack essential resources, I declare the crooked path is made straight, no more delay or disappointment. The Lord has gone ahead of me and shall expose to me the hidden and buried resources (Zechariah 4:9)

ASSIGNMENT

• Identify what you have given up on that you need to pick up again and continue with it again.

DAY 13

TELL ME ABOUT IT

PRAYER QUOTE:

"I surrendered unto him all there was of me, everything. Then for the first time I realized what it meant to have real power." - Kathryn Kuhlman

SCRIPTURE:

"I am the LORD, that is my name; and my glory I will not give to another, nor my praise to carved images. Behold, the former things have come to pass, and new things I declare; before they spring forth I tell you of them." (Isaiah 42:8-9)

To work in your FRESH START, you also need some fresh revelations, old things have passed away and something new is about to happen to you but first you need to hear the news!

It is important for you to know that you cannot operate in your FRESH START beyond the knowledge you have, or what you don't know. It is clearly stated in the scriptures, "My people are destroyed for lack of knowledge (Hosea 4:6) We remain limited by what we know or what we don't know. This means, one of the greatest limitations of humans is not the many things we may not have but the lack of knowledge. This is not so with the God whom we serve, for nothing is hidden before his face. He is All-knowing. The entire bible exposed the omniscience of God and the scripture says God declares even the end and the result from the beginning and from ancient times the things that are not yet done. (See Isaiah 46:10)

"Behold, the former things have come to pass, and new things I declare; before they spring forth I tell you of them." (Isaiah 42:8-9 NKJV)

"…before they spring forth I tell you of them." God is saying he will let us know about things and he would announce what will happen next, meaning before things happen in our life God will announce it. It's left to us to pay attention. Nothing happens by accident, it's just that we are not sensitive to catch God's frequency when he announces.

"I still have many things to say to you, but you cannot bear them now. 13 However, when He, the Spirit of truth, has come, He will guide you into all truth; for He will not speak on His own authority, but whatever He hears He will speak; and He will tell you things to come." (John 16:12-13)

These were the words of Jesus to His disciples assuring them that the Holy Spirit will guide them into all reality and that He will reveal to them things to come. In your season of Fresh Start, it is the desire of God to guide, guide you through revelations of things that had never being heard. (1 Corinthians 2:9-12)

The scripture says, *"The secret things belong to the LORD our God, but those things which are revealed belong to us and to our children forever, that we may do all the words of this law."* (Deuteronomy 29:29)

God has a blueprint and a counsel for your Fresh Start. In the scriptures, Saul's father lost his donkey, but God has already spoken to Samuel about it and even Saul's coming the night before. When Saul appeared, he knew because God spoke to him, letting him know this is the man I spoke to you about, meaning God can show you things, even tell you the woman or man that you would marry. God had already told Samuel where he would meet Saul and the things that he would do. Do you know God can reveal secrets to you on your job that can help your company, and bring you honor and favor from the boss? (1 Samuel 9-10)

God speaks, and we must learn how he speaks and to be sensitive to His voice and leadings.

Once you know the things that are to happen on the way, it will:

Enhance Your Focus: it will give you an edge to be able to focus and take right decisions due to the foreknowledge you have.

Grant You Grace For Intelligent Pursuit: when you know things that are to happen ahead of time, you will be able to intelligently pursue what God has revealed. It will enhance effectiveness and precision in your actions; especially in your dealing with people and your use of resources; you would not be guessing your way through. God didn't show Joseph that he was going to be head of the prisoners, but a prime minister.

It is important to be conscious of the fact that all revelations or inspirations must align with the integrity of God's written word so as not to fall into error. You must be willing and ready to give up any inspiration or revelation that does not agree with the character of the written word of God.

You may want to ask, how do I get the revelation? Revelations are caught in the place of prayer. Jeremiah 33:3 says, *"Call to Me, and I will answer you, and show you great and mighty things, which you do not know."* By prayer and supplication, God can reveal to you a secret recipe or formula or plan for your business. Ask great chefs or confectioner who by divine inspiration have had their recipes sought after, all over the world. What about inventors? Many inventions as a result, have fundamentally changed the course of human history. Through dreams or visions, the Spirit of God has taught many what to do.

God promised -

"And it shall come to pass afterward that I will pour out My Spirit on all flesh; your sons and your daughters shall prophesy, your old men shall dream dreams, Your young men shall see visions. 29 And also on my menservants and on My maidservants I will pour out My Spirit in those days." (Joel 2:28-29)

"Eye has not seen, nor ear heard, nor have entered into the heart of man the things which God has prepared for those who love Him. But God has revealed them to us through His Spirit. For the Spirit searches all things, yes, the deep things of God. 11 For what man knows the things of a man except the spirit of the man which is in him? Even so no one knows the things of God except the Spirit of God. 12 Now we have received, not the spirit of the world, but the Spirit who is from God, that we might know the things that have been freely given to us by God." (1 Corinthians 2:9-12 NKJV)

You are entering into a new phase of your journey in destiny, a Fresh Start, although you have not navigated that route before, there is someone who knows it all, He will guide you into all truth and show you things to come. And by the authority in the name of Jesus, every power behind your lack of promotion at work, or your late marriage will be exposed and disgraced. And the Lord will open your eyes to see the invisible and your ears to hear the inaudible, your heart will perceive and capture all required for your triumph in this season of Fresh Start, in Jesus name.

I decree that an end comes to struggling in any area of your life in Jesus mighty name. I decree and declare that the devourer that tends towards poverty in your life will be devoured in the mighty name of Jesus Christ. The counsel of the devil against you and your family will not stand. It will be exposed and destroyed in Jesus name.

The mind of God is given to men by Revelations so that we can be directed for action.

Fresh Start Gem: "All things are ordained of God and are settled by Him, according to His wise and holy predestination. Whatever happens here happens not by chance, but according to the counsel of the Most High! The acts and deeds of men below, though left wholly to their own wills, are the counterpart of that which is written in the purpose of Heaven." - Charles Spurgeon

✤

YOU MAY PLAN YOUR ACTIONS BUT GOD DIRECT YOUR STEPS!

PRAYER POINTS

• Father, I worship you EL DEAH, the God of Knowledge. Holy Spirit I want to hear you afresh. I want to hear the details of what the Father has for me. Help me to distinguish your voice from every other voice that may be speaking to me, By Your mercy, please LORD, speak to me in a plain language that I can easily understand and not in parables (1 Samuel 2:3; Matthew 13:13)

• Father, let my eyes become an instrument of divine visions; let my ears become your instrument of divine instructions, my heart the instrument of divine perceptions. Open my eyes to see the opportunities within my problems.

• Father, help me to see the invisible and do the impossible in the name of Jesus. Give me the grace to obey you totally no matter how inconvenient or unpopular (Psalm 1:6; Proverbs 3:5-6)

• Father shows me my destination; help me not to make a temporary place my permanent residence. I am holding onto Your Word, " I will point out the road that you should follow. I will be your teacher and watch over you" I know You will not just tell me what to do but also when to, how to, where to, and who to work with (Psalm 32:8; Ezekiel 20:6)

ASSIGNMENT

• Commit yourself more to prayers in the Holy Spirit. (Jude 20)

DAY 14

✤

RUNNING WITH A VISION

PRAYER QUOTE:

"Be specific in your prayer requests of God." - Benny Hinn

SCRIPTURE:

"And the Lord said to Abram, after Lot had separated from him: "Lift your eyes now and look from the place where you are — northward, southward, eastward, and westward; 15 for all the land which you see I give to you and your descendants forever." (Genesis 13:14-15)

Vision is seeing the future before it comes to be. Vision is the ability to see farther than your eyes can look. Vision is what we see, but it is also the way in which we see; that is your perception. While someone may be looking at a problem, the other person may be looking at an opportunity. I don't know what you may have gone through and may be going through but if you cannot see an opportunity of escape you may belong there. You must have a clear vision for your FRESH START. It is beyond mere sight. While all men who could see with their eyes wide open did not see the opportunity in Jesus; presence a blind man saw, and he got a restoration (Mark 10: 46 -52)Have an image of what you want, where you want to be and who you want to be. (Genesis 13:15 - 17) God told Abram before he became Abraham, after Lot had left him, "Lift up now your eyes and look at the place where you are, northward and southward and eastward and westward; For all the land which you see I will give to you and to your posterity forever:" Abraham looked with faith and saw beyond his physical surrounding. In like manner, before you receive anything from God you need to have seen it, you need to have captured it in the visions of your heart through your imagination.

To really enter into a season of a FRESH START, you must be able to see beyond what your eyes can look because what you see is what determines what you can obtain or attain. In our text, God told Abram to lift up his eyes and look *"for all the land which you see I give to you and your descendants forever"*. For Abram to obtain what God has in store for him, he must be able to see beyond his present circumstances. What you cannot see, you cannot possess. Abraham had to first see himself as the "Father of nations" before he actually became one.

In this season of Fresh Start, you need to start with a clear vision so you can pursue and experience God's best for your life, ministry, businesses, and all other areas of your life in which you desire a FRESH START.

Vision will help you to cut out distractions and waste; with the vision you will know where you are going, and you will be able to identify the route that will take you there. Vision will help you to choose your friends wisely; It's not everybody that was in your life before that needs to be in your life in your new season if they are not supporting your vision; you don't need such people. It's not everybody you carry from one season to another; Vision chooses our priorities; use of time, use of energy and use of resources. Vision determines your lifestyle, and life plan.

The Bible declares that *"Where there is no revelation, the people cast off restraint; but happy is he who keeps the law".* (Proverb 29:18)

Vision promotes self-discipline. A clear vision simplifies life, it narrows your options. Your vision can either build or destroy you. Without life is purposeless.

What actions are required for your vision?

[Oh, I know, I have been rash to talk out plainly this

way to God!] I will [in my thinking] stand upon my post of observation and station myself on the tower *or* fortress and will watch to see what He will say within me and what answer I will make [as His mouthpiece] to the perplexities of my complaint against Him. And the Lord answered me and said, Write the vision and engrave it so plainly upon tablets that everyone who passes may [be able to] read [it easily and quickly] as he hastens by. For the vision is yet for an appointed time and it hastens to the end [fulfillment]; it will not deceive *or* disappoint. Though it tarry, wait [earnestly] for it, because it will surely come; it will not be behindhand on its appointed day.

It comes from either God or You.

It must be written clearly and precisely.

You must be patient, it is a process and has time to its fulfillment, don't truncate it.

Your vision will need others to come into it.

Nehemiah in the bible was a man whom God placed in his heart to rebuild the wall of Jerusalem. He was a cupbearer to Artaxerxes, the king of Persia. (See Nehemiah 1:1) At the time the Babylon captivity, the city of Jerusalem had undergone serious destruction. After he heard that, he wept and for days he mourned, fasted, and prayed (Nehemiah 1:4) but he was able to see – beyond the present state of things-that the wall can be rebuilt. This was a vision for him, though many never saw that the wall could be rebuilt; but God laid it on his heart to build it. (See the book of Nehemiah). Vision precedes Passion.

The following steps will help to keep you on track in accomplishing your vision:

Step 1: Focus on Fewer Goals

Any goal takes effort – and tackling more than two or three at a time is beyond most of us. Rather than trying to change everything overnight, focus on just a couple of key goals. Ideally, you'll want to choose goals that complement one another.

For instance, if you're aiming to lose weight, you might have a secondary goal of getting more fit – the two goals work in tandem. If you're trying to write a book, though, it's probably not a good idea to also work on starting up a small business – you may not have enough hours in the day (or enough creative energy) for both goals.

Step 2: Plan Ahead

One reason why goals get derailed is that we fail to plan ahead. It's all too easy to use a string of social events as an excuse to give up on a diet, or to abandon a fledgling side business during a busy spell in the day job.

Take a look at your diary over the next month or so. Do you have anything coming up that's likely to cause problems for one of your goals? If you know you're going to be away for a long weekend, for instance, you might plan to do some work on your small business on weekday evenings instead. If your friend's going to throw a big birthday party, you may want to be extra-careful with your diet in the days immediately before and after.

Step 3: Set Milestones

Your goal might seem a very long way off right now. If you're aiming to lose 100lbs, or get a novel published, or have a full-time small business, you might be looking at months or years of work. At times, it'll feel as though your progress is slow.

Instead of focusing solely on the end goal, give yourself some milestones along the way. Celebrate every 5 lbs that you lose, or each finished section of your new book. Give yourself a deadline to aim for with each milestone – and make it achievable, but not unrealistic.

Step 4: Build Good Habits

Much of what we do in life is habitual. You probably don't need to constantly remind yourself to shower or brush your teeth or eat lunch – it's just a normal part of your day. When it comes to your goals, though, it might be a constant struggle to find the time or energy for them.

By developing good habits that support your goals, you'll find it much easier to make progress. For instance, if you struggle to find the time to exercise, try looking for a way to fit in into your day – perhaps by walking or cycling to work, or by doing some stretches during commercial breaks in the evenings.

Step 5: Track Your Progress

When you've been working on the same goal for a long time, it might feel as if you're not making much progress. If you look back to where you were a few months ago though, you'll often find that you've come a surprisingly long way.

Tracking your progress could mean keeping a journal, writing a list of key achievements each month, or recording particular statistics (like your weight or body fat percentage). It doesn't matter exactly how you go about tracking things – what matters is that you have some way to easily see what you've already achieved.

Step 6: Get Support and Encouragement

It's much easier to stay motivated when you have positive, supportive, people around you. Hopefully, you've got friends, family, or colleagues who can encourage you towards your goal – but it might be the case that these people don't understand why this is so important to you.

Look for a group that shares your goal: perhaps a writers' circle, a meet-up of self-employed professionals in your field, a dieting club, or a local gym, a fresh start group, empowerment group or any group coaching opportunities. This should provide you with the opportunity to meet like-minded people who can share your enthusiasm, and offer you advice, support, and encouragement.

What has the Lord laid on your heart to do, what are the dreams and visions he has caused you to see? Have you been stocked in a point and it seems as though you can't move further? Or you don't have a vision for life yet. Can we call on the Lord? The Holy Spirit is the revealer.

"Eye has not seen, nor ear heard, nor have entered into the heart of man the things which God has prepared for those who love Him." 10 But God has revealed them to us through His Spirit. For the Spirit searches all things, yes, and the deep things of God." (1 Corinthians 2:9-10)

Fresh Start Gem: "Life is not a dress rehearsal, stop practicing what you're going to do and just go do it. In one bold stroke you can transform today." - Marilyn Grey

❧

START! DON'T PROCRASTINATE

PRAYER POINTS

• Father, show me my destination. I refuse to settle for less than what you have for me. Remove any scale covering my eyes and melt any wax blocking my spiritual ears, and let every veil covering my heart blocking spiritual perceptions that could make miss out on your very best for me. I receive the seven anointing of the Holy Spirit. I shall not judge my what I, hear or sees but by the discerning of the Spirit (Psalm 25:4-5; Isaiah 11: 2-4)

• Father, you are the one that knows all things from the beginning to the end. According to your promise, I'm calling on you right now and I am asking that you please answer me and show me those marvellous and wondrous things about my Fresh Start that I can never figure out on my own (Jeremiah 33:3; Habakkuk 2:2-3)

• Father, show me the way to go about my journey, so I don't get to be weary, tired, or worn out; I stand upon Your promise, "I will the blind on roads they have never known; I will guide them on paths they have never travelled. Their road is dark and tough, but I will give light to keep them from stumbling. This is my solemn promise." (Ecclesiastes 10:15; Isaiah 42:16)

• Father, grant me wisdom and insight in decision making; and counsel for every step that I decided to take. Let every step I take lead me to peace and joy in the Holy Ghost (Proverbs 11:14)

• Father, connect me with those whom I can share my dreams and visions with for confirmation and encouragement. Divinely connect me to the right mentors, coaches and counselors . Disconnect from me vision hijackers, destroyers, and diverters. Help to guide my mouth and protect my vision (Acts 9: 10 -19; Proverbs 11:14)

• Father, grant me the speed and tenacity to complete my visions and goals to ensure my Fresh Start. Enable me to push forth and bring forth. I come against manifestation of failure at the edge of victory. I come against any manner of distraction from the pursuit of my vision either by accolade or criticism in the mighty name of Jesus (1 Kings 18:46; Hebrews 10:35-36)

ASSIGNMENT

• Write the vision, make it plain (simplify the vision).

• Share it with people who can encourage you about it and with those that are required to run with it.

• Run with the vision by taking steps to accomplish it.

• Be patient in accomplishing the vision because it will certainly come.

DAY 15

✤

TRAVEL WITH ME!

PRAYER QUOTE:

"Transformation comes in the end, not from an act of will but an act of grace, we can only ask for it and keep asking". – Philip Yancey

SCRIPTURE

Moses said, *"If your presence doesn't take the lead here, call this trip off right now. How else will it be known that you're with me in this, with me and your people? Are you traveling with us or not? How else will we know that we're special, I and your people, among all other people on this planet Earth?"* (Exodus 33:15-16)

"And Joseph was brought down to Egypt; and Potiphar, an officer of Pharaoh, captain of the guard, an Egyptian, bought him of the hands of the Ishmaelites, which had brought him down thither.² And the LORD was with Joseph, and he was a prosperous man; and he was in the house of his master the Egyptian. And his master saw that the LORD was with him, and that the LORD made all that he did to prosper in his hand. And Joseph found grace in his sight, and he served him: and he made him overseer over his house, and all that he had he put into his hand. And it came to pass from the time that he had made him overseer in his house, and over all that he had, that the LORD blessed the Egyptians house for Joseph's sake; and the blessing of the LORD was upon all that he had in the house, and in the field. And he left all that he had in Joseph's hand; and he knew not ought he had, save the bread which he did eat. And Joseph was a goodly person, and well favored." (Genesis 39: 1-6)

Travel with me is simply saying God, I need your presence, and I cannot do without you.

When God travels with you it marks you out and distinguishes you. "There is a factor, one that distinguishes a man from other men. It has nothing to do with his education or family pedigree. The factor that sets one apart from the masses is carriage of the presence of God. No one can ever remain the same once he has entered God's presence. No wonder Moses refused to do anything or go anywhere except he was certain that the presence of God is with him (Exodus 33:14-19) Those who came in contact with Joseph, such as Potiphar, Pharaoh, and the prison superintendent could not deny that there was something special about him.

The proof that the Israelites were his own special children was that God traveled with them; likewise, you also can only be distinguished wherever you go by his presence abiding with you.

Joseph was brought down to Egypt as a young man to serve Potiphar as a slave. The scripture shows us that he was in the house of his master, the Egyptian, and he was prosperous. And eventually in prison he was also a prosperous man. We see the secret to his prosperity in the passage below.

"And the LORD was with Joseph, and he was a prosperous man; and he was in the house of his master the Egyptian." (Genesis 39: 2)

There is beauty and power in God's presence. As you embark on this journey of a Fresh Start, you must understand the necessity of God traveling with you in this journey. Even the success of the earthly ministry of our Lord Jesus was attributed to God's presence abiding with him.

"How God anointed and consecrated Jesus of Nazareth with the (Holy) Spirit and with strength and ability and power; how He went about doing good and, (@)in particular, curing all who were harassed and oppressed by (the power of) the devil, for God was with Him." (Acts 10:38)

WHAT DO YOU STAND TO GAIN BY GOD TRAVELLING WITH YOU?

- It will be the secret of the success in your Fresh Start journey.

- It will be the key to your prosperity, as it will attract favor for you from the high and the mighty.

- It will transform you from just being a mere man into being a channel of blessings. It is the secret behind great exploits.

- God's presence in you will result in the fullness of joy.

- With God's presence traveling with you there is guaranteed victory, safety, protection, and security.

- With God traveling with you on this journey, you are assured of the successful safe landing of your Fresh Start.

- You are bound to have pleasures instead of pressures, fullness of joy instead of sadness, clarity instead of confusion, grace instead of disgrace, and honor instead of shame.

HOW DO YOU SECURE GOD'S PRESENCE?

You may ask, how do I secure his presence in my life continually? Psalm 16: 11 show us the beauty and power of his presence.

"You will show me the path of life; in Your presence is fullness of joy, at Your right hand there are pleasures forevermore." (Psalm 16: 11)

- We activate the presence of God through the atmosphere of prayers, meditation, and high praises. Prayer is you talking to God. It is the habit of finding quiet time with the intention of hearing from God. Prayer is not meant to solve problems alone. That is a major problem with our understanding of prayers, especially in Africa where I come from. We tend to pray only when we have problems and challenges. Prayer is a lifestyle and should be a habit. Imagine having a lover whom you don't talk to. What then is the essence of the relationship? That is it: *Relationship.* Prayer is the communication of an effective relationship. You communicate with God as the day goes by. You may pray while you are driving. Make prayer a lifestyle, have creative ways of praying. You may be passing through a street and decide to pray for the street and its inhabitants. The prayer approach many have towards God is that when there is troubles they cry out to God and when the troubles are solved they say Lord see you again next time. That is a sugar Daddy relationship and that approach has gotten many into trouble. It also prevented them from growing in faith and the knowledge of God and his son Jesus Christ. Prayer is essentially a relationship with God, not another religious activity.

- Make it a habit of finding quiet time with the

intention of hearing from him. Meditation is hearing from God, meditation is God communicating back to you as you ponder on His word.

"Don't get off track, either left or right, so as to make sure you get to where you're going. And don't for a minute let this Book of The Revelation be out of mind. Ponder and meditate on it day and night, making sure you practice everything written in it. Then you'll get where you're going; then you'll succeed. Haven't I commanded you? Strength! Courage! Don't be timid; don't get discouraged. God, your God, is with you every step you take." (Joshua 1:17-9)

• Be expectant of God's presence. Be expectant of His blessings

• Intense worship in spirit and truth (John 4:23-24)

• Become a mountaintop person. Rise above the noise of this world and hear from God. You have to form a habit of getting away from the crowd to continually secure his presence. Jesus was a perfect example of this. (Joshua 1:8; Mark 1:35)

"And in the morning, long before daylight, He got up and went out to a deserted place, and there He prayed. And Simon (Peter) and those who were with him followed Him ([1]pursuing Him eagerly and hunting Him out), And they found Him and said to Him, Everybody is looking for You." (Mark 1:35-37)

• Praises is extolling God for his mighty works and acts, it was a potent weapon for the children of Israel and it still unlocks heaven's blessings today. Worship God in spirit and in truth for He is holy and He inhabits the praises of his people. Your habitual praising of God literally creates an atmosphere of his presence around you. This makes it easy for God to move on your behalf. God seeks to move on behalf of those who worship him.

"But the hour cometh, and now is, when the true worshippers shall worship the Father in spirit and in truth: for the Father seeketh such to worship him.²⁴ God is a Spirit: and they that worship him must worship him in spirit and in truth." (John 4:23-24)

"Worship GOD if you want the best; worship opens doors to all his goodness." (Psalm 34:9)

Just like Moses, that presence is something you cannot afford to miss. You will need a higher power to deal with the overwhelming situations on the way or overbearing oppositions. You will get to the point that you might ask where God is. Situations that will want you to think like going back to whatever you may have left behind, especially when faced with surmounting problems, just as the children of Israel when they faced the Red Sea.

God is the one that promised to give you a Fresh Start in the first instance. He is committed to being with you throughout the journey.

"Let your character or moral disposition be free from love of money (including greed, avarice, lust, and craving for earthly possessions) and be satisfied with your present (circumstances and with what you have); for He (God) Himself has said, I will not in any way fail you nor give you up nor leave you without support. (I will) not, (I will) not, (I will) not in any degree leave you helpless nor forsake nor let (you) down (relax my hold on you)! (Assuredly not!)" (Hebrews 13: 5)

The fact that you have a promise from God does not mean there will be no opposition or problem. But you can be sure that God's presence is the equipment you need to surmount all oppositions. When Moses became adamant and hesitated in responding to God's assignment because of the trouble he foresaw in confronting Pharaoh, he insisted on God traveling with them. God's presence did not just assure him, but also granted him more benefits. So, His presence will give extra benefits, other than the comfort of his presence, there will also be a testimony of his presence on your behalf in signs and wonders.

"But I'll take the hand of those who don't know the way, who can't see where they're going. I'll be a personal guide to them, directing them through unknown country. I'll be right there to show them what roads to take, make sure they don't fall into the ditch. These are the things I'll be doing for them— sticking with them, not leaving them for a minute." (Isaiah 42:10-16)

The assurance of his presence with us should embolden

us to take the bull by the horns and move towards the realization of our God-given dream.

WHAT DO YOU STAND TO LOSE WITHOUT GOD'S PRESENCE?

- Your divine ordained blessings

- Divine fellowship

- Divine instructions

Fresh Start Gem: "You will never win if you never begin." - Helen Rowland

❦

DON'T BE ON YOUR OWN

PRAYER POINTS

• JEHOVAH SHAMMAH, I thank you for your presence. I bless You for the promise of Your constant and continuous presence. I am grateful for this kindness and Your faithfulness. (Isaiah 43:1-4)

• Father, please have mercy on me for any way I have not followed you wholly or wandered from your presence. I confess and repent of any entanglement with anything that is unproductive and ungodly. I refuse to go back to my vomit (2 Peter 2:20 -22; Genesis 4:16; Isaiah 59:2 Proverbs 14:12; 1 John 1:9)

• Father, like Moses, I crave your presence, for my Fresh Start rests on it. Without you that journey will be in struggle. Make me a carrier of your presence; a presence that brings unusual success and prosperity in all projects and assignments and in every sphere of my life. Let your presence be evident and tangible. Let your presence magnetize unsolicited blessings from unsolicited sources. Genesis 39:2 -4,21 -23; Acts 10:38)

• Father, let me never go to where you will never go with me, do what you will never sanction or say what will never give you pleasure. And I know Your eyes are too pure to behold evil (Genesis 4:16; Habakkuk 1:13)

• Father, stride ahead of me in all battles and challenges physical, spiritual, visible, or invisible that may attempt to stall my Fresh Start (Isaiah 45:1-3)

• O Lord, draw me close, to you and take my hand on this journey according to Your Word, "Draw near to God, and He will draw near to You." (Isaiah 42:10-16; James 4:8)

ASSIGNMENT

• Write down exactly what you are expecting from God so that you can monitor and take note of your progress during the year.

• Take some time every day and give quality praise to God for the things you have listed down as expectations from him.

DAY 16

OUT OF THE DITCH

PRAYER QUOTE:

"The devil smiles when we make plans. He laughs when we get too busy. But he trembles when we pray, especially when we pray together." - Corrie ten Boom

SCRIPTURE:

"He said: The Lord is my Rock [of escape from Saul] and my Fortress [in the wilderness] and my Deliverer; My God, my Rock, in Him will I take refuge; my Shield and the Horn of my salvation; my Stronghold and my Refuge, my Saviour—You save me from violence. I call on the Lord, Who is worthy to be praised, and I am saved from my enemies. For the waves of death enveloped me; the torrents of destruction made me afraid. The cords of Sheol

were entangling me; I encountered the snares of death. In my distress I called upon the Lord; I cried to my God, and He heard my voice from His temple; my cry came into His ears." (2 Samuel 22: 2-7)

To be in the Ditch is to be in distress. Distress is anything that brings pain, suffering, misery, or sadness. It could be wretchedness, desolation, and despair. When David was getting away from Saul the bible says everyone in distress, in debt, and discontented gathered themselves to David and he became a commander over them. With him were about 400 men and David got away and escaped to the cave of Adullam. Everyone connected to his family came down and joined him. These men had needs and came to David; they started from nothing; they started as nobody and they ended up becoming mighty men of valor. It doesn't matter where you are on the journey of destiny, God can elevate you and accelerate your progress in the name of Jesus. Later on, in scriptures we read of these men. The Bible shows us how their destinies had taken a turn for good.

"Now these are they that came to David to Ziklag, while he yet kept himself close because of Saul the son of Kish: and they were among the mighty men, helpers of the war. They were armed with bows, and could use both the right hand and the left in hurling stones and shooting arrows out of a bow, even of Saul's brethren of Benjamin." (1 Chronicles 12: 1-2)

Do not despise anyone, even people around you whom you feel they are helpless or are nonentities.

Things can turn around for their good in a second. Those who came to David didn't come as men that could help David, they were in distress at that time and David cried unto God. In his distress he cried that the Lord should bring him out of the ditch. No matter the situation, don't think you are alone. Your crisis is not a surprise to God and before your crisis came, he made a provision and a solution available. Before the famine broke out God already provided a brook for Elijah. When it dried up God staged a comeback. The solution was already in God's hand. You might never know how God will sort you out and turn your situation around, you may never figure it out and God may not use conventional means.

"For my thoughts are not your thoughts, neither are your ways my ways, saith the LORD." (Isaiah 55: 8)

Could anyone have thought that a woman who had nothing and was oblivious to the community could have gotten such a visitation from God through the Prophet Elijah and overnight become a very wealthy woman? The woman had nothing, and was living from hand to mouth; yet, God said to Elijah that he had made provision for him in the house of a woman who had nothing, a widow. That's why you need God's instruction because his way of bringing you help may not be conventional. That is why it is crucial to focus on hearing from God, not just hanging out with men. They were both in need and God was connecting all the people in need together and meeting all their needs. We need to hand over the matter to the master planner, he will show us the way out of the ditch, you might not understand it, but he would walk you through as long as you are willing to follow in Faith. Remember the scripture says:

"If ye be willing and obedient, ye shall eat the good of the land." (Isaiah 1: 19)

When God has earmarked you for a Fresh Start, what you have might just be what is needed. The woman had only a little food, Elijah had the anointing for multiplication, but he needed something to begin with. God brought both of them together and something unimaginable happened. God is capable of bringing you in contact with people that will complement the skill that you have, he is able to connect you with helpers of destiny, people who will join you in running with the vision that God has given you. But many times we despise people, not knowing that the person we are looking at maybe the person we are looking for.

It happened in the Church that I attend, a guy was looking for a particular person for some business transaction and had failed seeing the person after many attempts, but unknown to him he had been sitting beside the same person in church every Sunday. Fortunately in a discussion with the Pastor, he mentioned his struggle to see a particular person in his office and when he mentioned the name, the Pastor told him, the person attends this church and sent for the person, lo and behold, it was the same guy they had been sitting next to each other. The moral of the story is, be nice, be courteous, be generous to other people.

The greatest hindrance to our elevation is our being full of ourselves. We must realize we are mere mortals dealing with the Immortal One. When we come to the place of emptiness, nothingness, and helplessness, God can then pick us up on his shoulders. You are not an independent and self-sufficient being.

"Know ye that the LORD he is God: it is he that hath made us, and not we ourselves; we are his people, and the sheep of his pasture." (Psalm 100:3)

There is wisdom from God still available to you today. God can bring you out of any ditch in life into a land flowing with milk and honey, but wisdom is essential to know his principles of operation.

GOD'S WISDOM FOR ENGINEERING A FRESH START FROM THE DITCH.

• Firstly, understand that your crisis is not a surprise to God! And before your crisis surfaced, he has made the solution available. Before the outbreak of famine, God already made Brook Cherith to provide the water and the ravens he had commanded to provide food. Before Brook Cherith dried up, God already stationed a widow. Today, hand over your situation to the master planner, He will show you the way out. Please note, whenever something unexpected happens, learn to respond calmly. God is never taken by surprise! (1 Kings 17)

"If your heart is broken, you'll find God right there; if you're kicked in the gut, he'll help you catch your breath." (Psalm 34:18 MSG)

• God's solution may not be conventional, it may not always make sense to the human logic, but what do you care? Think about it, what sense is there in using a hungry and famished Prophet Elijah to multiply food in the hand of a famished and dying woman, now that's God sense, it is uncommon. Get it. Glory to God!

• Secondly, you need to identify the areas where you need change, so you can monitor the progress you make as you affirm your faith in God in these areas. i.e. Financial, emotional, mental, marital, ministerial. You need to be exact in your appraisal of your situation and articulately express before the Lord God.

"Then the Lord instructed Moses, "Write this into a permanent record, to be remembered forever, and announce to Joshua that I will utterly blot out every trace of Amalek." (Exodus 17: 14)

• Thirdly, Express it. Speak out. Hannah was in a ditch of childlessness and was mocked by Peninnah continually. Hannah cried for years but nothing happened until she decided to articulately express her desire for a change to God. She prayed a very well-defined prayer to God once and God answered her. It is not enough to cry. Crying can't change situations, God does. The woman with the hemorrhage approached Jesus; she was in serious distress physically, emotionally, socially, and financially (1 Samuel 1:13-1; Mark 5:25 -34)

Asking is the principle to behind receiving.

"Ask, and you will be given what you ask for. Seek, and you will find. Knock, and the door will be opened. [8] For everyone who asks, receives. Anyone who seeks, finds. If only you will knock, the door will open." (Matthew 7: 7-8)

Jesus assured us in scripture, he said:

"You haven't tried this before, but begin now. Ask, using my name, and you will receive, and your cup of joy will overflow." (John 16: 24)

So, what are you waiting for, begin asking now!

- Fourthly, act: *"Action without vision is only passing the time, vision without action is merely day dreaming, but vision with action can change the world." – Nelson Mandela.*

After you have prayed and planned you must act. God moves on behalf of those who take steps in obedience to his promptings. You need to take actions in faith, and there is no telling what your steps of faith can accomplish. A beautiful illustration of this is found in this passage.

"Now there were four men with leprosy sitting at the entrance of the city gates. "Why should we sit here waiting to die?" they asked each other. "We will starve if we stay here, but with the famine in the city, we will starve if we go back there. So we might as well go out and surrender to the Aramean army. If they let us live, so much the better. But if they kill us, we would have died anyway."

So at twilight they set out for the camp of the Arameans. But when they came to the edge of the camp, no one was there! For the Lord had caused the Aramean army to hear the clatter of speeding chariots and the galloping of horses and the sounds of a great army approaching. "The king of Israel has hired the Hittites and Egyptians to attack us!" they cried to one another. So they panicked and ran into the night, abandoning their tents, horses, donkeys, and everything else, as they fled for their lives. When the men with leprosy arrived at the edge of the camp, they went into one tent after another, eating and drinking wine; and they carried off silver and gold and clothing and hid it." (2 Kings 7: 3-8)

Fresh Start Gem: "A time comes when you need to stop waiting for the man you want to become and start being the man you want to be." - Bruce Springsteen

❈

START TO MAKE EFFORT TOWARDS YOUR CHANGE

PRAYER POINTS

• Father, I lift my voice to give You praise, thank You, because You are bringing me out of that ditch. You are a shield around me, My glory and the one who lifts my head high (Psalm 3:3; Genesis 35:3)

• Father, open my eyes to wherever I might have gone astray, that made the devil able to afflict me. Search me, O God, and know my heart; test me and know my anxious thoughts. Point out anything in me that offends You and lead me in the path of everlasting life *(Psalms 119:67; 125:2; 139:23-24; Ecclesiastes 10;8)*

• Father, please give me a Fresh Start and help me keep alert to your righteous way. Deliver me from all my fears. Those who look to You for help will be radiant with joy; no shadow of shame will darken their faces; turn my shame to fame, turn my troubles to testimony, save me from them all. *(2 Samuel 22:21-25; Psalm 34)*

• Father, give me back my health and make me live again, make me healthy and strong again. Let me fully recover with a fresh infusion of life. Let me experience full restoration in the mighty name of Jesus. Like my testimony be like Job's, for it was written, "And the LORD restored Job's losses when he prayed for his friends. Indeed, the LORD gave Job twice as much as he had before. (Isaiah 42:22; Jeremiah 30:16-17)

• Father, I thank you because your light floods my path. Please drive out any darkness in my life. Enable me to smash the bands of marauders and vault the high fences in my way. I command a change to every negative situation in my life. I command every battle to convert to blessings; I command every evil confrontation to crumble. I bind the strongman of financial distress, emotional distress, marital distress, ministerial distress and I command you lose your hold on any area of my life now in the mighty name of Jesus. (2 Samuel 22:29-31; Psalm 84: 6 Matthew 18:18)

• Father, please equip me with strength for the battle; make those who rise against me sink under me. I gain dominion and I subdue all forces spiritual and physical by the power of the Holy Ghost. I declare and confess boldly: every opposition is converted to promotion, every ridicule is converted to miracle, every trial to testimony. (2 Samuel 22:40-47; Psalm 18:43-46)

ASSIGNMENT

• Write down all the definite steps you have taken concerning that situation in the past and evaluate them prayerfully.

• Prayerfully outline three action steps you are being inspired to take concerning that pressing situation and begin to take them by faith.

DAY 17

✦

THE ERASER AND THE MAGNET

PRAYER QUOTE:

"*Trouble and perplexity drive me to prayer and prayer drives away perplexity and trouble.*" - Philip Melanchthon

SCRIPTURE:

"*Therefore, since these (great) promises are ours, beloved, let us cleanse ourselves from everything that contaminates and defiles body and spirit, and bring (our) consecration to completeness in the (reverential) fear of God*". (2 Corinthians 7:1)

Many times we find a contradiction in our lives, there is a strong pull in our hearts towards something really great, yet when we try to reach towards it we seem to never be able to, so we are left frustrated. When you consider the story of Jabez for instance. Jabez had a measure of success but he could not attain a higher success because something was defiling, polluting, terminating, and negating the advancement of his destiny. There was a limiting factor in the life of Jabez. There was something that had bound him up. He had a desire to be better than his current state. He knew that there was more to his life than he was currently experiencing. This hindrance was a curse upon his life that he had carried from birth and was limiting him. Yet Jabez overcame his limitations, and the Bible testified that Jabez was more honorable than all his brethren. (I Chronicles 4: 9-10)

Another example was Ruth the Moabites, who was in the genealogy of Jesus. Ruth was also a cursed woman, she was an accursed person not by her own mistake but because of her ancestors as she was a Moabites; yet she desired to enter into a Fresh Start in life. Naomi, her mentor, told her to wash and anoint herself and put on her best clothes.

"Then Naomi her mother-in-law said to Ruth, My daughter, shall I not seek rest or a home for you, that you may prosper? Wash and anoint yourself therefore, and put on your best clothes and go down to the threshing floor, but do not make yourself known to the man until he has finished eating and drinking." (Ruth 3: 1, 3)

An evil pronouncement can pollute one's destiny, curses have plagued some families for many generations. A curse may be hidden, unknown but you can see the symptoms or the manifestations. An example of a curse in the scripture is that of Jacob upon his son Reuben (Genesis 49:3 -4) Curse is a stopper, places an embargo on a person's movement. A curse must be broken. The effect stays from generation to generation until it is destroyed, and its effect cancel. Apart from inherited curses, there are curses by association, by virtue of marriage or relationship or self-induced curse, this is curse provoked by a person. For example, when a man or woman is disappointed and places a curse on the other person. A lady I know was experiencing a delay in marriage and fortunately a word of knowledge came forth that there was an aunt who disappointed a guy and the man placed a curse upon all the girls in that family. She inquired and she found out the truth and the curse was broken. Now she is married. And that is why you need revelations in this journey of a FRESH START.

Now that you are a Christian in that family it is not enough for you to say that I am a Christian and I go to church, if you don't appropriate the blessings that God has given you in Christ Jesus you will continue to be a victim of Satan. If you are given a check and you don't cash it, it will remain in the bank, even though you have a promissory note.

There are also evil marks placed upon the destinies of men. The same way there could be divine marks placed on a man's life. That is why Paul said:

"From henceforth let no man trouble me: for I bear in my body the marks of the Lord Jesus". (Galatians 6: 17)

This meant his life had attracted trouble and evil, and his declaration here was directed to any principality or persons that sought to assault his life and destiny. He unequivocally made it clear that henceforth they no longer had the liberty to assault him because he bore on his body the marks of the Lord Jesus. This referred to his increased ranking of authority in the kingdom of God which came as a result of a life sold out to God.

TAKING INVENTORY OF THINGS THAT MUST BE ERASED FROM YOUR LIFE.

- Recurring negative patterns:

If you are observant you might notice a recurring evil trend in your family. These are demonic strongholds that attempt to dominate every member of the family. I know of a family where every third child in that family died. If someone does not arise in faith and put a stop to these things, they go unchallenged and continue in their tyrannical rule. For some families it could be a recurring pattern of delay in childbirth and you must rise up an erase it using the authority that you have in Christ Jesus. For some it's a spirit of disappointment and rejection that has been plaguing members of their family. A pattern of being almost there, but not getting to the desired end.

"And saviors shall come up on mount Zion to judge the mount of Esau; and the kingdom shall be the LORD's." (Obadiah 1: 21)

- Sin:

Sin is in the lives of many and is a recurring phenomenon. Sometimes as a result of wrong mindsets and wrong belief systems, the devil gains a foothold into the lives of many, locking in the bondage to negative habits and outlooks on life. They struggle to gain the freedom to no avail because they have not truly submitted to the Lordship of the Word in their lives. The moment they submit to the Lordship of the Word in their heart, they find that fellowship with God becomes easier and fun, and darkness bows out of their lives at the entrance of true light.

"But if we walk in the light, as he is in the light, we have fellowship one with another, and the blood of Jesus Christ his Son cleanses us from all sin." (1 John 1: 7)

Some negative patterns are habits, sickness, repeated failures, misfortunes and setbacks, poverty, defeat and bondage.

WHAT CAN ERASE THESE NEGATIVE PATTERNS?

- The Word of God:

"That he might sanctify and cleanse it with the washing of water by the word, That he might present it to himself a glorious church, not having spot, or wrinkle, or any such

187

thing; but that it should be holy and without blemish." (Ephesians 5: 26-27)

You will need to devotedly study and meditate on God's word. God's word is a powerful sanctifier. It is a most potent weapon of warfare for dislodging evil deposits in our lives.

"For the word of God is quick, and powerful, and sharper than any two-edged sword, piercing even to the dividing asunder of soul and spirit, and of the joints and marrow, and is a discerner of the thoughts and intents of the heart." (Hebrews 4: 12)

When doubts try to sneak up on you, you declare the word with confidence and affirm that you are washed in the blood of Jesus Christ and that you are triumphant in Christ Jesus.

- The Blood:

The blood of Jesus is an eraser. The blood of Jesus is the primary weapon to destroy the devil. The blood is a hedge against the destroyer.

"And they overcame him by the blood of the Lamb and by the word of their testimony; and they loved not their lives unto the death." (Revelation 12: 11)

The blood of Jesus redeems:

"And the blood shall be to you for a token upon the houses where ye are: and when I see the blood, I will pass over you, and the plague shall not be upon you to destroy you, when I smite the land of Egypt." (Exodus 12: 13)

188

- The Anointing:

The anointing is a magnetizer, it magnetizes good things. In Psalm 23: 5, the scriptures say, "He anointed my head with fresh oil." So, the oil is perfume and it magnetizes good things.

Anointing is also yokes and burden destroyers, so you need anointing to destroy. It does not matter how long your cursed or the problem had stayed. The anointing of the Holy-ghost can break every curse and any chain or shackle that might have kept you in bondage.

"And it shall come to pass in that day, that his burden shall be taken away from off thy shoulder, and his yoke from off thy neck and the yoke shall be destroyed because of the anointing." (Isaiah 10:2)

The anointing is also a lubricant which helps a person do what ordinarily that person would not have been able to do. It is a lubricant that God uses to spur us into great heights in life to the amazement of onlookers.

The anointing announces a man out of obscurity into the fulfillment of destiny. The anointing came upon David when he was in the desert and the anointing moved him into the frontline of life.

"I have found My servant David; With My holy oil I have anointed him, With whom My hand shall be established; Also My arm shall strengthen him." (Psalms 89:20-21)

The anointing helps to protect a man; it gives him the ability to enjoy his new level in the midst of his enemies.

"When they went from one nation to another, from one kingdom to another people, He permitted no one to do them wrong; Yes, He rebuked kings for their sakes, Saying, "Do not touch my anointed ones, and do my prophets no harm." (Psalm 105:13-15)

There is no doubt that you need the anointing for your FRESH START, just like Ruth.

For the Word, the Blood and the Anointing to work effectively:

• It is imperative that you intentionally flee from every sin and appearances of evil in and around your life. You cannot afford to keep the devil's works with you and expect the Lord to have free course to work in your life.

"Abstain from evil (shrink from it and keep aloof from it) in whatever form or whatever kind it may be." (1 Thessalonians 5:22)

• Secondly, you must be totally committed to God and to His word, it must become your daily delight, you must pay attention to God and fill your heart with His word.

"Meditate upon these things; give thyself wholly to them; that thy profiting may appear to all." (1 Timothy 4:15)

• Your number one priority must be the will of God. You must diligently seek to know his will for you per-time. This way you can be assured that his anointing will work for you because you are at the center of God's will.

"I delight to do your will, O my God; yes, your law is within my heart." (Psalms 40: 8)

• You also need faith in the Word of God, faith in the blood of Jesus, faith in the Anointing of the Holy Spirit is your part to play. As you go into deeper prayer, have faith in these three factors.

Fresh Start Gem: "If you want to live in the fullness of God's anointing, fill your mouth with His Word." - Joyce Meyer

✢

You need the WORD, the BLOOD, the OIL

PRAYER POINTS

• Father, I thank you for my redemption through the blood of Jesus. I thank you because in the name and the blood of Jesus I have overcome Satan; therefore, I have outstanding victory in every situation by the blood of the Lamb. I confess that I overcome any attack of the enemy against me. I overcome every negative and contrary situation in my life. Every contrary and negative situation shall work in my favor by the blood of Jesus, I shall no longer be defeated in the mighty name of Jesus. I shall no longer suffer from the effects of any curse in my life. I am the head and not the tail, above only and not beneath. I walk in favor, I walk in dominion, I walk in power, I walk in prosperity and

I walk in peace. By the power in the blood of the Lamb, I declare, God is my defender and I don't have defend myself against any accusation. I am unaccusable because of the blood, I am justified and acquitted, (Revelation 12:11; Galatians 3:13; Romans 5:9)

• Father, by your mercy let every defiling and polluting agent in my life be destroyed, Prepare me a sanctuary for you, pure and holy, tried and true (2 Corinthians :7:1)

• Father, let the blood of Jesus erase any evil mark upon my life attracting rejection, disappointment, and frustration in Jesus name. (Galatians 6:17)

• Anointing that destroys yokes and burdens fall on me, let every yoke be destroyed, let every burden be eliminated. I Revoke every evil, ungodly right of ownership upon my life and declare the ownership and Lordship of the Lord Jesus Christ (Isaiah 10:27)

• I Silence every voice speaking against the manifestation of my breakthrough and a FRESH START with the blood of Jesus, the blood of sprinkling that speaks better things than that of Abel I declare I am free from any old covenant that may have held me back and put me in any bondage. I have entered into a new covenant with better promises. (Hebrews 12:24; Isaiah 54:17)

My FRESH START is not negotiable; my story is changing, I'm going up, I'm moving forward, no curse can hold me back anymore, the power of sin is defeated, bad and evil habits and patterns are a thing of the past. It is a new day for me. HALLELUJAH!

ASSIGNMENT

• Write down all the definite steps you have taken concerning that situation in the past and evaluate them prayerfully.

• Prayerfully outline three action steps you are being inspired to take concerning that pressing situation and begin to take them by faith.

DAY 18

ATTITUDE MATTERS

PRAYER QUOTE:

"There are two kinds of people; those who say to God, "Thy will be done," and those to whom God says, "All right then, have it your way." - C.S. Lewis.

SCRIPTURE:

"But my servant Caleb - this is a different story. He has a different spirit; he follows me passionately. I'll bring him into the land that he scouted and his children will inherit it." (Numbers 14:24)

"Different Spirit" rendered in The Message Bible could also mean 'different attitude'.

The question here is, "What attitude will guarantee and sustain your Fresh Start. It is often said that your attitude determines your altitude. Some attitudes are needful to secure and sustain your Fresh Start.

So, the question to ask yourself now is, "What kinds of behavior is expected of me to experience a Fresh Start in my life?

The first point is your response towards instructions you're being given, a negative response towards divine or human instruction is indicative of the results you will see. Those who get excellent results are those who always respond positively, that is, responding in faith to whatever instruction you have been given. Your response is a reflection of the orientations you have received in life. These orientations, positive or negative, determine how prepared you are for your Fresh Start. Your opinions, ideas, convictions, feelings and thoughts could help or hinder your Fresh Start.

"[Inasmuch as we] refute arguments and theories and reasonings and every proud and lofty thing that sets itself up against the [true] knowledge of God; and we lead every thought and purpose away captive into the obedience of Christ (the Messiah, the Anointed One)." (2 Corinthians 10:5)

Let us consider a classic story of a man who could have bungled his Fresh Start by a negative attitude:

"Naaman was general of the army under the king of Aram. He was important to his master, who held him in

the highest esteem because it was by him that God had given victory to Aram: a truly great man, but afflicted with a grievous skin disease. It so happened that Aram, on one of its raiding expeditions against Israel, captured a young girl who became a maid to Naaman's wife. One day she said to her mistress, "Oh, if only my master could meet the prophet of Samaria, he would be healed of his skin disease." Naaman went straight to his master and reported what the girl from Israel had said. "Well then, go," said the king of Aram. "And I'll send a letter of introduction to the king of Israel." So he went off, taking with him about 750 pounds of silver, 150 pounds of gold, and ten sets of clothes. Naaman delivered the letter to the king of Israel. The letter read, "When you get this letter, you'll know that I've personally sent my servant Naaman to you; heal him of his skin disease." When the king of Israel read the letter, he was terribly upset, ripping his robe to pieces. He said, "Am I a god with the power to bring death or life that I get orders to heal this man from his disease? What's going on here? That king's trying to pick a fight, that's what!".

Elisha the man of God heard what had happened, that the king of Israel was so distressed that he'd ripped his robe to shreds. He sent word to the king, "Why are you so upset, ripping your robe like this? Send him to me so he'll learn that there's a prophet in Israel." So Naaman with his horses and chariots arrived in style and stopped at Elisha's door.

Elisha sent out a servant to meet him with this message: "Go to the River Jordan and immerse yourself seven times.

*Your skin will be healed and you'll be as good as new."
Naaman lost his temper. He turned on his heel saying,
"I thought he'd personally come out and meet me, call on
the name of God, wave his hand over the diseased spot,
and get rid of the disease. The Damascus rivers, Abana
and Pharpar, are cleaner by far than any of the rivers in
Israel. Why not bathe in them? I'd at least get clean." He
stomped off, mad as a hornet.*

*But his servants caught up with him and said, "Father,
if the prophet had asked you to do something hard and
heroic, wouldn't you have done it? So why not this simple
'wash and be clean'?" So he did it.*

*He went down and immersed himself in the Jordan seven
times, following the orders of the Holy Man. His skin
was healed; it was like the skin of a little baby. He was as
good as new."* (2 Kings 5:1-14)

Naaman got his attitude right, responded positively,
and consequently received a Fresh Start of his healing.

WHAT IS THE NEGATIVE ATTITUDE THAT COULD DEPRIVE YOU OF YOUR FRESH START?

PRIDE

Pride is the major negative attitude that will deprive
you of your Fresh Start. Pride could be manifested in
many ways, two of which are:

- Trying to fully understand the method and way

that God has purposed to affect your Fresh Start before you believe Him.

"I don't think the way you think. The way you work isn't the way I work." God's decree. "For as the sky soars high above earth, so the way I work surpasses the way you work, and the way I think is beyond the way you think. Just as rain and snow descend from the skies and don't go back until they've watered the earth, Doing their work of making things grow and blossom, producing seed for farmers and food for the hungry, So will the words that come out of my mouth not come back empty-handed. They'll do the work I sent them to do, they'll complete the assignment I gave them." (Isaiah 55:8-11)

• Despising the people in your Fresh Start, not knowing that He in his wisdom has chosen to put his treasure in an earthen vessel, that the Excellency of the power might be of God and all glory should go to God:

"[No] for God selected (deliberately chose) what in the world is foolish to put the wise to shame, and what the world calls weak to put the strong to shame. And God also selected (deliberately chose) what in the world is lowborn and insignificant and branded and treated with contempt, even the things that are nothing, that He might depose and bring to nothing the things that are, So that no mortal man should [have pretense for glorying and] boast in the presence of God." (1 Corinthians 1:27-29).

WHAT ATTITUDES DO YOU NEED TO EXHIBIT FOR A FRESH START?

• HUMILITY

"He guides the humble in what is right and teaches them his way." (Psalm 25:9)

You must be humble to receive help from others and to receive counsel from others. Naaman demonstrated humility when he received counsel from a servant girl. Be humble to receive support from others and to get information from others that might be beneficial to our Fresh Start.

"When Moses' father-in-law saw all that he was doing for the people, he said, what is this that you do for the people? Why do you sit alone, and all the people stand around you from morning till evening? Moses said to his father-in-law, because the people come to me to inquire of God. When they have a dispute they come to me, and I judge between a man and his neighbor, and I make them know the statutes of God and His laws. Moses' father-in-law said to him, the thing that you are doing is not good. You will surely wear out both yourself and this people with you, for the thing is too heavy for you; you are not able to perform it all by yourself. Listen now to [me]; I will counsel you, and God will be with you. You shall represent the people before God, bringing their cases and causes to Him." (Exodus 18: 14-19)

- ## TRUST GOD AND TRUST HIS METHOD.

"Lean on, trust in, and be confident in the Lord with all your heart and mind and do not rely on your own insight or understanding. In all your ways know, recognize, and acknowledge Him, and He will direct and make straight and plain your paths." (Proverbs 3:5-6)

The widow of Zarephath never questioned the process of God. She responded to the negative situation in Obedience and Faith. (1 Kings 17:8-16)

- ## FIND A COUNSELLOR, BE CONNECTED AND STAY CONNECTED

Follow through with counsels from trusted counselors, stay connected and focused.

"He that walketh with wise men shall be wise: but a companion of fools shall be destroyed." (Proverbs 13: 20)

- ## DILIGENCE

"Whatever your hand finds to do, do it with all your might, for in the realm of the dead, where you are going, there is neither working nor planning nor knowledge nor wisdom." (Ecclesiastes 9:10)

- ## PASSION AND EXCELLENCE

"But Ruth said, "Don't force me to leave you; don't make me go home. Where you go, I go; and where you live, I'll live. Your people are my people, your God is my god; where you die, I'll die, and that's where I'll be buried, so help me God —not even death itself is going to come between us!" (Ruth 1:16-17)

You have to be passionate about what you feel strongly about and apply yourself to an excellent pursuit of it.

"Whatever your passion is, do it to the best of your ability. Do it to the fullest. Follow it wherever it leads you. Follow it passionately. You have no idea what awaits you on the other side. That passion will lead you to your destiny. When your instinct merges with passion, you get your destiny." - T. D. Jakes

- SUBMISSION

Submission to God and constituted authority and instruction is essential.

"In your relationships with one another, have the same mindset as Christ Jesus: Who, being in very nature God, did not consider equality with God something to be used to his own advantage; rather, he made himself nothing by taking the very nature of a servant, being made in human likeness. And being found in appearance as a man, he humbled himself by becoming obedient to death— even death on a cross!" (Philippians 2:5-8)

- FAITH INSTEAD OF FEAR

"And Jesus, replying, said to them, Have faith in God [constantly]. Truly I tell you, whoever says to this mountain, Be lifted up and thrown into the sea! And does not doubt at all in his heart but believes that what he says will take place, it will be done for him. For this reason I am telling you, whatever you ask for in prayer, believe (trust and be confident) that it is granted to you, and you will [get it]." (Mark 11:22-24)

- FORGIVENESS AND LETTING GO.

One way the enemy is keeping you back from entering and enjoying your Fresh Start is to keep you in the trap of bitterness and unforgiveness. Do I say it is easy, I can preach on this, but you have to just let go for your own sake!

"Get rid of all bitterness, rage and anger, brawling and slander, along with every form of malice. Be kind and compassionate to one another, forgiving each other, just as in Christ God forgave you." (Ephesians 4:31-32)

"Joseph was a man who did not allow bitterness from the past to hold him back; despite the betrayal he received from his brothers when they met again he simply told them, "You meant it for evil, but God meant it for good." (Genesis 45:5 -8)

- SACRIFICE

A FRESH START will also require some sacrifice, that is giving up on some rights, loved things, long time relationships, and habits. For a person dieting, the box of chocolates in the refrigerator may have to go, time for other things that may be assigned to your FRESH START.

"Sometime later God tested Abraham. He said to him, "Abraham!" "Here I am," he replied. Then God said, "Take your son, your only son, whom you love —Isaac — and go to the region of Moriah. Sacrifice him there as a burnt offering on a mountain I will show you." (Genesis 22:1-2)

- ## COURAGE INSTEAD OF GUILT

You need the courage to take action of your convictions. We are often settled in contrary situations or places because we lack the courage to make a move towards achieving our goals.

"Don't be afraid, for I am with you. Don't be discouraged, for I am your God. I will strengthen you and help you. I will hold you up with my victorious right hand." (Isaiah 41:10)

We are afraid of getting out of the familiar for the unfamiliar. We all crave for safety, that desires have killed many dreams and truncated many goals. My high school principal would often say then, "nothing ventured, nothing gained".

- ## COMPANY

There are times you cannot do it alone. You may need accountability, encouragement, and sometimes you need to be challenged by the company of great men who will inspire and challenge your attitude. Ruth and Naomi formed a formidable team. For instance, the Alcoholics Anonymous has what is known as a "buddy system".

Fresh Start Gem: "Let go of yesterday. Let today be a new beginning and be the best that you can, and you'll get to where God wants you to be." - Joel Osteen.

❋

ATTITUDE DOES MATTER

PRAYER POINTS

• Father, help me to please you, appealingly conducting myself. Show me Your way, O LORD and teach me Your paths. Lead in Your truth as I embark on this journey of FRESH START. Teach me, for You are the God of my salvation and I wait on You. (Psalm 25:4-5)

• Father, release to me the grace to be submissive, humble, forgiving, and obedient. I receive the garment of humility; for You resist the proud and give grace to the humble. Let me be guided by integrity. (1 Peter 5:5 -6; Proverbs 11:3)

• Father, help me with my character, in dealing with character flaws.

• Search me [thoroughly], O God, and know my heart! Try me and know my thoughts! And see if there is any wicked or hurtful way in me and lead me in the way everlasting. (Psalm 139:23-24)

• Father, thank you for launching me into my season of Fresh Start. Help me to pursue my goal with a passion to the fullest that may indeed fulfill destiny.

ASSIGNMENT

• Is there anyone who contributed to any set back you have experienced? Forgive them completely without any reservation.

DAY 19

✣

CLINGING

PRAYER QUOTE:

"Prayer should be the key of the day and the lock of the night." - George Herbert

"And they lifted up their voice, and wept again: and Orpah kissed her mother in law; but Ruth clave unto her. And she said, Behold, thy sister in law is gone back unto her people, and unto her gods: return thou after thy sister in law. And Ruth said, entreat me not to leave thee, or to return from following after thee: for whither thou goest, I will go; and where thou lodgest, I will lodge: thy people shall be my people, and thy God my God: Where thou diest, will I die, and there will I be buried: the LORD do so to me, and more also, if ought

but death part thee and me. When she saw that she was steadfastly minded to go with her, then she left speaking unto her." (Ruth 1:14-18)

Naomi left where she was staying and moved to another place because of recession and she lost all. Then, she desired a Fresh Start and she desired to go back to where she came from. Sometimes we have to go back to where the ax head fell. So, she told the daughter-in-laws that she wanted to go back and they began to follow her.

When you decide to move forward and to start afresh, or to do something that is new, aside from the status quo, there will be voices and people who will tell you there is no way you can achieve your aim.

While Ruth was determined to leave the cursed land of Moab and start something new, her well-meaning mother-in-law insisted that Ruth should not follow her. She didn't know where she was going or what was going to be waiting for her, but Ruth said I need to go.

Naomi resisted, but Ruth was determined. There is a season where you will not accept no for an answer despite the opposition. People will tell you no way, circumstances will tell you no way, but you need to hold on to your dream. It's not that they have bad intentions, but their perception, or their opinion is based on what they can see. If you have your information from the God who can do all things, and who knows the future, then there will be a stirring in your spirit that tells you that you cannot go back, you must advance, and you must make more of an impact, and expand your sphere of influence.

There is a program that I am convening by the word of God. I do it because I failed somewhere, and I said I would not allow anybody else under my influence to make that kind of mistake. The young ones love the program and they love to know 'a nobody' is telling them things about life.

There was nobody in the past that made it through that did not have someone or something discouraging them, usually to hold on to the pursuit of their goals; a scriptural example was The Blind man who resisted all attempts to stop him from receiving help from Jesus. (Mark 10:46 -52) No matter the odds, no matter who may be fighting against you, you will not give up or go back.

There are obstacles to the journey into your Fresh Start that needs to be dealt with or else they will become stoppers of your destiny. Take note that not every rejection is a loss, a man rejected Ruth. There are many kinds of obstacles and things that will attempt to stop you. There are self-induced stoppers, Man-induced stoppers, Demonic induced stoppers, and Environmental induced stoppers.

CERTAIN THINGS CAN STOP ONE FROM GAINING HIS FRESH START.

- The Battle of the Mind:

"What shall we then say to these things? If God be for us, who can be against us? He that spared not his own Son, but delivered him up for us all, how shall he not with him also freely give us all things? Who shall lay anything to the charge of God's elect? It is God that justifieth.

Who is he that condemneth? It is Christ that died, yea rather, that is risen again, who is even at the right hand of God, who also maketh intercession for us. Who shall separate us from the love of Christ? Shall tribulation, or distress, or persecution, or famine, or nakedness, or peril, or sword?

As it is written, For thy sake we are killed all the day long; we are accounted as sheep for the slaughter. Nay, in all these things we are more than conquerors through him that loved us.

For I am persuaded, that neither death, nor life, nor angels, nor principalities, nor powers, nor things present, nor things to come, Nor height, nor depth, nor any other creature, shall be able to separate us from the love of God, which is in Christ Jesus our Lord." (Romans 8: 31-39)

Our mind is one of our most potent tools for our success. But an un-renewed and weak mind is also the devil's tool against a man.

- Accusations:

Accusations I have observed usually go before a FRESH -START, Think of Joseph (Genesis 39) Daniel (Daniel 6) The Hebrew Trio (Daniel 3) Accusation goes before godly elevation or promotion. When you experience that, know the end of suffering is near. In all those cases, they held onto their faith and their God and their God came through for them just as he would come through for you in the mighty name of Jesus.

The demonic accusation can be expressed in various ways in the life of an individual, which usually results in various abnormalities, such as depression. Etc. An example of demonic accusations/oppression was King Saul of Israel.

"But the Spirit of the LORD departed from Saul, and an evil spirit from the LORD troubled him." (1 Samuel 16: 14)

• Condemnation:

This happens when men use what they know about you to confront or attack you. It is a weapon of discouragement. Don't fall for that trick. You should know, "Therefore, there is now no condemnation for those who are in Christ Jesus." Most time run with half the story about you. You know the true story, especially if you have been divorced before.

A friend was in a Bible class and the other women were not sensitive enough in their utterances saying things like, "If you were divorced it means you are not good." She came out of that meeting crying. Most times people don't know the full story but are judgemental. Men may condemn you but don't condemn yourself for God has not condemned you. What condemnation does is to confine you?

A man called Job experienced a terrible set back and his friends condemned him and his wife convinced him to curse God and die (Job 2:9) Job did not yield and eventually God gave him a FRESH START and it was recorded, "And the LORD blessed the latter days of Job more than his beginning…" (Job 42:12)

- Discouragement:

Discouragement can come through the actions or inactions of others. Ruth could have followed the action of her sister-in-law, but she followed her own path. If you don't believe and follow something you will fall for anything. Determine what you want and follow through regardless who believes you or not. Cling to your dreams and goals.

"Then they wept aloud again; and Orpah kissed her mother-in-law (good-bye), but Ruth clung to her. And Naomi said, See, your sister-in-law has gone back to her people and to her gods; return after your sister-in-law. And Ruth said, urge me not to leave you or to turn back from following you; for where you go I will go, and where you lodge I will lodge. Your people shall be my people and your God my God. Where you die I will die, and there will I be buried. The Lord do so to me, and more also, if anything but death parts me from you. When Naomi saw that Ruth was determined to go with her, she said no more." (Ruth 1:14-18)

Despite all the excuses Naomi gave to discourage Ruth from following her to Bethlehem, Ruth was determined not to allow anything to stand in the way of her Fresh Start.

When you are determined to make a Fresh Start there will be many voices of discouragement, even from well-meaning people, but like Ruth you must know how to say no, she clung to Naomi.

To Cling means to hold on tightly to, clutch, grip, grasp, clasp, attach oneself to, hang on to, embrace, hug.

THE PRICE FOR CLINGING

- FOCUS:

The focus is an important price to pay to keep clinging on to God or your destination. Without a focus on Jesus, Peter began to sink, he could no longer cling. Likewise, we, when we lose our focus, might begin to sink.

"And Peter answered him and said, Lord, if it be thou, bid me come unto thee on the water. And he said, Come. And when Peter was come down out of the ship, he walked on water, to go to Jesus. But when he saw the wind boisterous, he was afraid; and beginning to sink, he cried, saying, Lord, save me. And immediately Jesus stretched forth his hand, and caught him, and said unto him, O thou of little faith, wherefore didst thou doubt?" (Matthew 14: 28 - 31)

- STRONG DESIRE:

Ruth had a strong desire for a FRESH START and she was determined to have it. In your Fresh Start journey you will encounter many obstacles and without a strong desire you will easily loosen your grip.

Fresh Start Gem: "Desire is the starting point of all achievement, not a hope, not a wish, but a keen pulsating desire which transcends everything. In order to succeed, your desire for success should be greater than your fear of failure." - Anonymous

❖
NO MATTER THE ODDS DON'T GIVE UP!

PRAYER POINTS

• Father, thank You for my FRESH START, I know there are situations and people along the way that could cause some discouragement and distractions, please teach me the strategy and the wisdom to deal with any of such as it comes. (Proverbs 24:3 -4; James 1:5)

• Father, teach me the strategy to Fight the battle of my Fresh Start and subdue every opposition known and unknown, visible and invisible, spiritual and physical in any department of my life.

• Father, arise and contend with every contender of my FRESH START in the mighty name of Jesus (Isaiah 49: 23-26)

• Father, I hope in You and I place my full and unswerving trust in You. Thank You for always giving me the courage to be strong; I receive afresh courage instead of discouragement for my FRESH START. I declare I am strong, for You are the strength of my life; therefore I will be afraid of anyone or any situation that may suddenly appear against me or my goal. I'm resolute, expectant, and hopeful for a great turn around (Psalm 31:23-24; Psalm 7:1; 1 Samuel 4:9; Ezekiel 2:6)

• I refuse to allow anything or anyone to distract me, even the good things that are not important or needful for my FRESH START. I resist discouragement and resistant and I come against the operation and activities of such spirit in my life. Father, whatever it will take You increase my resolve to wholly follow the path You have charted for my FRESH START, and grant me the grace to follow through in the mighty name of Jesus (John 14:1)

ASSIGNMENT

• How strong is your desire for a Fresh Start?

• Enumerate five key areas of distraction and begin to prayerfully confront them.

DAY 20

❧

CONQUER THE GIANTS

PRAYER QUOTE:

"If you are too busy for prayer you are too busy for a relationship with God." - Mike Bickle

SCRIPTURE:

"Now they departed and came back to Moses and Aaron and all the congregation of the children of Israel in the Wilderness of Paran, at Kadesh; they brought back word to them and to all the congregation, and showed them the fruit of the land. Then they told him, and said: "We went to the land where you sent us. It truly flows with milk and honey, and this is its fruit. Nevertheless the people who dwell in the land are strong; the cities are fortified and very large; moreover we saw the descendants

of Anak there. The Amalekites dwell in the land of the South; the Hittites, the Jebusites, and the Amorites dwell in the mountains; and the Canaanites dwell by the sea and along the banks of the Jordan." Then Caleb quieted the people before Moses, and said, "Let us go up at once and take possession, for we are well able to overcome it." But the men who had gone up with him said, "We are not able to go up against the people, for they are stronger than we." And they gave the children of Israel a bad report of the land which they had spied out, saying, "The land through which we have gone as spies is a land that devours its inhabitants, and all the people whom we saw in it are men of great stature. There we saw the giants (the descendants of Anak came from the giants); and we were like grasshoppers in our own sight, and so we were in their sight." (Numbers 13:26-33)

When spies were sent out to view the land that God promised the children of Israel as an inheritance, they met Giants who were called the children of Anak and a majority of them were greatly afraid. Majority of the spies sent out said the feat was impossible, but Caleb and Joshua had a different Spirit in them, it was the Spirit of a conqueror. These are the type of people who are able to conquer the Giants.

In every land of promise there are always giants:

"For we are not fighting against people made of flesh and blood, but against persons without bodies-the evil rulers of the unseen world, those mighty satanic beings and great evil princes of darkness who rule this world; and against

huge numbers of wicked spirits in the spirit world.

So use every piece of God's armor to resist the enemy whenever he attacks, and when it is all over, you will still be standing up." (Ephesians 6:12-13)

Who do you see, God or giants? If you see God you will be unstoppable, if you see giants, you will be stopped. If you focus on He who can do exceedingly abundantly above all that you can ask or think, who is able to strengthen you against all oppositions that might come your way.

David was a man who faced several trials and persecution and he went through a very long wilderness journey, even after he was anointed as king. King Saul was seeking to kill him, but God, in his infinite mercies, kept him and made him triumphant at the end.

Here is what he said about the dealing he had with God:

"He teacheth my hands to war; so that a bow of steel is broken by mine arms." (2 Samuel 22:35)

Here he was testifying the goodness and greatness of God, and he said that God taught his hands to war and now his arms can bend a bow of steel. This statement was a spiritual one carrying a deep meaning that God had taught him how to face and overcome the oppositions and the giants that were situated in his promised land.

Many Problems arise on the border of the promised land.

- Inferiority complex

"There we saw the giants (the descendants of Anak came from the giants); and we were like grasshoppers in our own sight, and so we were in their sight." (Numbers 13:33)

See what Job said to his own opposition:

"Yes, I've seen all this with my own eyes, heard and understood it with my very own ears. Everything you know, I know, so I'm not taking a backseat to any of you. I'm taking my case straight to God Almighty; I've had it with you—I'm going directly to God. You graffiti my life with lies. You're a bunch of pompous quacks! I wish you'd shut your mouths— silence is your only claim to wisdom." (Job 13:1-5)

- **Curses** from men like Balak and Balam who wanted to overturn the blessings of the children of Israel. (Numbers 22; 23)

- **Silent operators** will be in the form of household enemies like Absalom, who was David's son, yet wanted to topple his father. Absalom led a rebellion against his father, after he had charismatically and politically won the favor of the people governed by his father. Their story you can find in the book of 2 Samuel chapter 13 through chapter 18. It is the story of people who are very close to you; you can call them unfriendly friends or pretentious enemies.

They seem to be in supportive of your FRESH START but secretly working against it. Have you ever heard the phrase "The fifth Columnist" A fifth columnist is anyone who secretly supports and helps the enemies against external forces. Your discernment to discover such people and disconnect from them. I had a bitter experience of such and I can tell it, it can be devastating and destructive.

• **Bosses or Leaders:** These are people who are your leaders, supervisors, in the church or on the job who are expected to help you rise, but instead are envious of your expertise, talents, and gifts. Therefore, instead of promoting you or helping, they sabotage your efforts and undermine or rubbish your contribution just to discourage you. We saw for many years how King Saul pursued David to destroy him despite David's trust and submission to Saul (2 Samuel 3:1) One major point you must bear in mind is that when you focus on God your giants will fall, when you focus on giants you will fall. David became a giant killer because he was able to apply that basic wisdom, even at a tender age. Don't focus on your negative circumstances or challenges to your FRESH START but focus on God who can make it happen.

"And when the Philistine looked about and saw David, he disdained him; for he was only a youth, ruddy and good-looking. So the Philistine said to David, "Am I a dog that you come to me with sticks?" And the Philistine cursed David by his gods. And the Philistine said to

David, "Come to me, and I will give your flesh to the birds of the air and the beasts of the field!" Then David said to the Philistine, "You come to me with a sword, with a spear, and with a javelin. But I come to you in the name of the Lord of hosts, the God of the armies of Israel, whom you have defied. This day the Lord will deliver you into my hand, and I will strike you and take your head from you. And this day I will give the carcasses of the camp of the Philistines to the birds of the air and the wild beasts of the earth, that all the earth may know that there is a God in Israel. Then all this assembly shall know that the Lord does not save with sword and spear; for the battle is the Lord's, and He will give you into our hands." So it was, when the Philistine arose and came and drew near to meet David that David hurried and ran toward the army to meet the Philistine. Then David put his hand in his bag and took out a stone; and he slung it and struck the Philistine in his forehead, so that the stone sank into his forehead, and he fell on his face to the earth." (1 Samuel 17:42-49)

It was a war of words and David prevailed because he didn't look at the size of the philistine, but the size of his God. His victory came because he believed in a God able, willing, and ready to lift him above his enemy. The scriptures says, in Hebrews chapter 12 and verse 2, "Looking unto Jesus, the author and finisher of our faith, who for the joy that was set before Him endured the cross, despising the shame, and has sat down at the right hand of the throne of God."

So, stop looking at your problems, instead fix your

eyes on the one who is able to solve your problems and who is capable of turning your problems to opportunities.

That same God will lift you and catapult you into your Fresh Start in Jesus Name.

Past failure should not be excuse enough not to pursue your desired Fresh Start. Failure should be a source of motivation to press for victory. You have not failed unless you quit.

The Psalmist said:

"Remember me, Lord, when you show favor to your people; come near and rescue me. Let me share in the prosperity of your chosen ones. Let me rejoice in the joy of your people; let me praise you with those who are your heritage." (Psalms 106:4-5)

Other giants we might likely face are:

- National Environmental threat (Esthonians 3:8)

- Glory terminators (Matthew 2: 13)

- Discouragers (Mk.10:46-52)

Fresh Start Gem: "Life takes on meaning when you become motivated, set goals and charge after them in an unstoppable manner." –Les Brown

❧

INSTEAD OF LOOKING AT WHAT, START AT LOOKING AT WHO!

PRAYER POINTS

• Father, thank You for the place and position you have mapped out for me; the one You have searched out, discovered and explored, the land that is flowing with milk and honey, the best of all lands anywhere, the one I know of and the one I'm yet to know about. I receive the grace to continue my journey in destiny and I refuse to stop before I reach my destination (Ezekiel 20:5-6)

• Father, keep me thirsting for more of You; the more of You I see and the more of You I have the less of problems and giants I see. Please let anything that would constitute a giant in my upward journey be removed by fire in the name of Jesus (Psalm 63: 1-3; Matthew 3:10; 15:13)

• Father, let everything in me waiting to rob me or stop me be destroyed. Grant me a new and right spirit or attitude like Caleb. I receive the grace to push past the pain and the gain of yesterday to press towards the mark for the prize of my FRESH START.

• I condemn every evil tongue speaking against my recovery, restoration, breakthroughs, and success. I come against any activity of darkness to stop me before I reach my goal. I refuse and reject any satanic substitute for my destiny. I shall not miss my goal and destination in Jesus name. I declare I'm pressing higher (Isaiah 54:17; Philippians 3:14)

• Father, let my life, ministry, marriage, family, business, career be a testimony of your glory and power. Let my testimony shock and disappoint my detractors. Make a way to turn my story to glory and let Your grace terminate every disgrace and shame in my life in the mighty name of Jesus

ASSIGNMENT

• Note every giant within or without and write down strategies as inspired to tackle and eliminate.

DAY 21

❈

IT SHALL COME TO PASS!

PRAYER QUOTE:

"People are drawn to prayer because they know that God's power flows primarily to people who pray." - Bill Hybels

SCRIPTURE:

"And Jesus answered them, Truly I say to you, if you have faith (a firm relying trust) and do not doubt, you will not only do what has been done to the fig tree, but even if you say to this mountain, Be taken up and cast into the sea, it will be done." (Matthew 21: 21)

In these past 21 days, you have prayed for many things, which means that you will have the things that you have spoken of (Isaiah 65:24) Believe that it is done.

When I ran this program originally with some people in the Transformational Prayers Network, I heard on the last day, just as I was about to enter into the virtual prayer room, "Not just that I would do a new thing, but the new you shall emerge." When God was done with Saul, people were asking if he was now all of a sudden a Prophet, which would mean God will make you outstanding among many people and they would see the Glory of God upon you. What God wants to do in your life is to help you create a new you, transform your life and change your story for His glory. The bible says in Romans 8 and verse 28, "And we know with great confidence that God who is deeply concerned about us, causes all things to work together as a plan for good for those who love God, to those who are called according to His plan and purpose."

When Naaman came out the waters, after his healing the bible said his flesh was new like a child. (2 Kings 5:14) God is set to do something amazing in your life that will draw men's attention, making you a signature of God's glory and power, a new you is coming forth in the name of Jesus. (Psalm 126)

And I think I'm already testimony in this regard; recently people have been telling me you're looking different and suddenly one day I remembered this prophecy, the Bible's account of Hannah is an inspiring one. It was recorded that immediately she finished prayer and the prophet gave the assurance of answered prayer, her countenance changed, she was no longer sad.

"So Hannah rose up after they had eaten in Shiloh, and after they had drunk. Now Eli the priest sat upon a seat by a post of the temple of the LORD. And she was in bitterness of soul, and prayed unto the LORD, and wept sore. And she vowed a vow, and said, O LORD of hosts, if thou wilt indeed look on the affliction of thine handmaid, and remember me, and not forget thine handmaid, but wilt give unto thine handmaid a man child, then I will give him unto the LORD all the days of his life, and there shall no razor come upon his head.

And it came to pass, as she continued praying before the LORD, that Eli marked her mouth. Now Hannah, she spake in her heart; only her lips moved, but her voice was not heard: therefore Eli thought she had been drunken. And Eli said unto her, How long wilt thou be drunken? Put away thy wine from thee. And Hannah answered and said, No, my lord, I am a woman of a sorrowful spirit: I have drunk neither wine nor strong drink, but have poured out my soul before the LORD. Count not thine handmaid for a daughter of Belial: for out of the abundance of my complaint and grief have I spoken hitherto.

Then Eli answered and said, Go in peace: and the God of Israel grant thee thy petition that thou hast asked of him. And she said, Let thine handmaid find grace in thy sight. So the woman went her way, and did eat, and her countenance was no more sad. And they rose up in the morning early, and worshipped before the LORD, and returned, and came to their house to Ramah: and Elkanah knew Hannah his wife; and the LORD remembered her." (1 Samuel 1:9-19)

As you continue you must know that there are necessary steps that need to be taken towards the actualization of what you believe in God for, those are the actions you must take, the places you have to go, and ensure that you do the appropriate.

The woman with the issue of blood determined to have her Fresh Start and she got it. (Mark 5: 25 - 34) A woman of Canaan desired a Fresh Start for her daughter who had been sick, and she got one. (Matthew 15: 21 -28) Elisha desired and determined in his ministry to operate in a higher dimension of his calling and anointing and he got one. (2 Kings 1: 1- 14) Blind Bartimaeus determined to have a Fresh Start from being a beggar to his sight being restored, he got what he desired. (Mark 10:46 -52)

Delay is not denial, God has a plan for your delay, remember that it came to pass concerning Hannah. IT SHALL COME TO PASS FOR YOU TOO!

She came back later for her testimony and you too shall come back to share your testimony very soon. (Isaiah 51:10) Listen to her testimony:

"For this child I prayed; and the LORD hath given me my petition which I asked of him: Therefore also I have

lent him to the LORD; as long as he liveth he shall be lent to the LORD. And he worshipped the LORD there." (1 Samuel 1: 27-28)

REQUIREMENTS TO BRING IT TO PASS:

1. PRAY.

Prayer terminates problems and launches you into a season of fresh start.

Don't just sit down looking at your situation, enjoying pity parties. While the parties were enjoying themselves in Jairus house he secretly went through another to go and meet Jesus to save his dying daughter. (Mark 5) Arise to do something about your situation, leave the pity party, leave the mockers, secretly go into your closet and call on your Father, He is waiting for you. (James 4:1-4; Matthew 7:7; Jeremiah 29: 10 -13; John 14-14; Jeremiah 33:3; Isaiah 65:24) Hannah's Fresh Start was to be a mother.

"There was a man named Elkanah who lived in Ramah in the region of Zuph in the hill country of Ephraim. He was the son of Jeroham, son of Elihu, son of Tohu, son of Zuph, of Ephraim. Elkanah had two wives, Hannah and Peninnah. Peninnah had children, but Hannah did not." (1 Samuel 1:1-2 NLT)

Hannah prayed and took action.

"Once after a sacrificial meal at Shiloh, Hannah got up and went to pray. Eli the priest was sitting at his customary

place beside the entrance of the Tabernacle. Hannah was in deep anguish, crying bitterly as she prayed to the Lord. And she made this vow: "O Lord of Heaven's Armies, if you will look upon my sorrow and answer my prayer and give me a son, then I will give him back to you. He will be yours for his entire lifetime, and as a sign that he has been dedicated to the Lord, his hair will never be cut." (1 Samuel 1:9-11 NLT)

"So it came to pass in the process of time that Hannah conceived and bore a son, and called his name Samuel, saying, "Because I have asked for him from the Lord." (I Samuel 1:20)

2. HAVE FAITH.

Don't pray but add to your prayer faith. (1 John 5:14-15)

Then Jesus told them:

"I tell you the truth, if you have faith and don't doubt, you can do things like this and much more. You can even say to this mountain, 'May you be lifted up and thrown into the sea,' and it will happen. You can pray for anything, and if you have faith, you will receive it." (Matthew 21:21-22)

3. BELIEVE GOD HAS THE LAST WORD OVER YOUR LIFE AND NOT THE DEVIL.

There is always a termination date for every trouble, for every situation, and for distress and yours has come. NO MORE...

"The suffering won't last forever. It won't be long before this generous God who has great plans for us in Christ— eternal and glorious plans they are! —will have you put together and on your feet for good. He gets the last word; yes, he does." (1 Peter 5:810-11)

4. DON'T JUST SEEK FOR HELP, BUT SEEK FOR HELP IN THE RIGHT PLACES AND IN THE RIGHT WAYS.

The help of man is useless, limited and unreliable compared with the help of God. (Psalm 60:11;108:12; 146:3; Judges 5:23)

The question is, who are you consulting for your Fresh Start? Who are you looking up to? Rachael, Jacob's beloved wife desired a Fresh Start but was going about it in the wrong direction. She was looking up to the wrong person, her husband, a mere mortal who has tons of issues and character flaws that needed to be addressed. (Genesis 32: 22 -32)

"Now when Rachel saw that she bore Jacob no children, Rachel envied her sister, and said to Jacob, "Give me children, or else I die!" And Jacob's anger was aroused against Rachel, and he said, "Am I in the place of God, who has withheld from you the fruit of the womb?" (Genesis 30:1-2)

Until Rachel went to God nothing happened, but it came to pass for her when she did and it was recorded later in Genesis chapter thirty and in verses twenty two and twenty three "Then God remembered Rachel, and

God listened to her (You have to speak for somebody to listen) and opened her womb. And she conceived and bore a son, and she said," God has taken away my reproach."

As you call on God in this season, May He listen to you, answer you and take away everything in your life that has brought shame to you and to His name.

5. DONT TRY FIXING YOUR ISSUES YOUR OWN WAY, BUT IN GOD'S WAY.

Trying to fix it your way can complicate issues for you and others on the long run.

Till date there is trouble in Palestine because of the singular act of self - prescribed solution by Sarah

"Now Sarai, Abram's wife, had borne him no children. And she had an Egyptian maidservant whose name was Hagar. So Sarai said to Abram, "See now, the Lord has restrained me from bearing children. Please, go in to my maid; perhaps I shall obtain children by her." And Abram heeded the voice of Sarai. Then Sarai, Abram's wife, took Hagar her maid, the Egyptian, and gave her to her husband Abram to be his wife, after Abram had dwelt ten years in the land of Canaan. So he went in to Hagar, and she conceived. And when she saw that she had conceived, her mistress became despised in her eyes." (Genesis 16:1-4)

Ask for the grace to grace wait patiently for your change to come like Job. (Job 14:14)

James similarly advised thus:

"Consider it a sheer gift, friends, when tests and challenges come at you from all sides. You know that under pressure, your faith-life is forced into the open and shows its true colours. So don't try to get out of anything prematurely. Let it do its work so you become mature and well-developed, not deficient in any way." (James 1:2-4)

GOD HAS A PLAN FOR EVERY DELAY:

It may not have come to pass for you to have that testimony hitherto because the answers to your requests and the fulfillment therefore are attached to a divine timing and purpose. (Luke 1:20) Believe! You are a carrier of great destiny and potentials awaiting great delivery! (Habakkuk 2:2-3) It will surely come to pass. Behold it came to pass for Hannah and testified:

"For this child I prayed, and the Lord has granted me my petition which I asked of Him. Therefore I also have lent him to the Lord; as long as he lives he shall be lent to the Lord." So they worshiped the Lord there." (I Samuel 1:27-28)

PERFECTION: THE END GOAL.

After you may have suffered awhile, after your patience through trials and tribulation, God intends to bring you to perfection and establish you in every aspect of your life. God's dream is to grant you total wholeness, perfection in relationships, the perfection of health, and perfection of your walk with God.

To establish is to make a position or condition firm and stable; causing growth and multiplication, with the element of permanency and security. When you place your life in the hands of God, he will not just take you out, contrary to the situation and abandon you in the middle but will settle you in a definite destination. He will bring you to perfection and establish you in the land, in your marriage, business, health; many sickly, but God is set to bring yours out of every health challenge, career, and ministry. Etc. Hallelujah.

"I took a solemn oath that day that I would bring them out of Egypt to a land I had discovered and explored for them—a good land, a land flowing with milk and honey, the best of all lands anywhere." (Ezekiel 20:6 NLT)

SPIRITUAL PERFECTION

"Make you perfect in every good work to do his will, working in you that which is well pleasing in his sight, through Jesus Christ; to whom be glory forever and ever. Amen." (Hebrews 13:21)

"For it is God which worketh in you both to will and to do of his good pleasure." (Philippians 2:13)

God will also bring you to Spiritual perfection or maturity. This however cannot be achieved using flesh. God forges us and sometimes purifies in trials and battles which are not to break us but to mold us. The trials come to pass but the beauty and perfection it fashions in our hearts remains forever.

WHEN YOU PLACE YOUR LIFE AND HOPE IN GOD'S HANDS HE IS SURE TO BRING YOUR STORY TO A REASONABLE CONCLUSION

As you place the broken pieces of your life into God's strong and mighty hands, I don't have any doubt that your story comes to a reasonable conclusion. You will not just have a FRESH START but your story shall end well. God will give result hat cancel insults. You shall have an answer to silence mockers, Your trials shall turn to testimony.

FRESH START GEM: "Imperfection and perfection go so hand in hand, and our dark and our light are so intertwined, that by trying to push the darkness or the so-called negative aspects of our life to the side... We are preventing ourselves from the fullness of life."
- Jeff Bridge

❖

AND IT SHALL COME TO PASS. DON'T ABORT THE PROCESS

PRAYER POINTS

• Father, to You, I give all the praise, let my life be used for Your glory. Thank You for bringing me to the end of this program. Perfect all that concerns me - emotional, marital, ministerial, physical, mental, financial, and spiritual. I command the spirit of infirmity to lose your hold upon my life.

I claim and receive total healing in all areas of my life. I receive the touch of God for total healings and restoration (Exodus. 15: 26)

• Father, please repair and rebuild every faulty foundation that may pose a threat to my Fresh Start in Jesus name. I pull down all the faulty foundations: environmental and ancestral strongholds (Psalms 11: 3; Matthew 7:24-25)

• Father, let there be a performance of Your Word in my life. Now is the time for manifestation. I receive the strength to bring forth. Now Lord, reveal your glory and power upon me and through me by notable miracles and breakthroughs (Jeremiah 1:12; Isaiah 55:10 -11)

• Father, empower my hands to finish that which you have started through me and anoint me to receive that which you have started for me in Jesus name. (Zechariah 4: 6,9; Ps.89:20-29).

• Father, please supply me the speed and tenacity to complete my visions and goals to ensure my Fresh Start. Enable me to push forth and bring forth. I shall not lack anything good and beneficial to my FRESH START I declare boldly- No more miss, no more diversion, no more diversion, no more detour, no more denial, no more defection, no more deferment, no more delay, no more failure, no miscarriage but manifestations, success, breakthroughs, promotions, prosperity, victory, and jubilation (1 Kings 18:46; Isa. 40:29-31)

ASSIGNMENT

• List in your journal, what are your areas of expectations, even in trying times?

• What actions are you expected to take on your part? God will not do your part for you.

• Be specific, if you are not specific you cannot measure the outcome.

CLOSING WORDS

Having gone through a season of disappointment, rejection, and abuse setbacks, emotionally, financially, socially and getting back on your feet was not fun; but, I eventually did. And like David, I placed the pieces of my life into His hands and through a series of prayers I discovered a lot of things to deal with and I can tell you it is not easy to do by yourself sometimes. That's why you need a personal coach.

Contact Coach Treasure!

BOOK YOUR FREE 15 MINUTES
STRATEGIC SESSION NOW

www.damolatreasureokenla.com

Praise God for a FRESH START in that area of life where you most desire it. You asked and you received, but the most important FRESH - START anyone can have is that FRESH START with God. Right now, you can submit to His Lordship and Leadership if you have never done that and if you have once before done so, but now alienated yourself from Him because of your negative situation, you too can also come back to Him. He is eagerly waiting to rebuild you and your dreams. (Jeremiah 31:3-4)

It does not matter what you have done or how far you have fallen and regardless your past, God's specialties includes making a 'nobody' into a ' somebody' significant and 'something' out of 'nothing' in order to transform lives and situations, Listen to this :

"Take a good look friend at who you were when you got called into this life. I don't see many of "the brightest and the best" among you, not many influential, not many from high-society families. Isn't it obvious that God deliberately chose men and women that the culture overlooks and exploits and abuses to choose these "nobodies" to expose the hollow pretensions of the "somebodies"? (1 Corinthians 1: 26 -28)

Jesus is in the business of giving people a Fresh Start. The apostle Peter says, "Because Jesus was raised from the dead, we've been given a brand-new life, and have everything to live for, including a future in heaven." (1 Peter 1:3-4)

So today, why don't you just stop and confess to Him as your LORD and Saviour.

It is a simple prayer:

> ### Dear God,
>
> *I know I'm a sinner and I ask for your forgiveness, I believe that Jesus Christ is Your son. I believed that He died for my sin and that you raised him to life. I want to trust Him as my Saviour and follow Him as my LORD. From this day forward*

grant me a brand new life and a FRESH START in Christ Jesus. Guide my life and help me to do Your will no matter how seemingly hard it may be. I pray this in the mighty name of Jesus. Amen. (John 3:16; John 10:10; Romans 3:23; 6:23; 5:8' 1 Corinthians 15:3-4)

THE BEST IS YET TO COME!

WHAT TO DO

1. COME TO JESUS. HANDOVER YOUR LIFE AND SITUATION TO HIM. I believe you have done that by the prayer you prayed earlier on. Matthew 11:28-29; Proverbs 3:5-6; Psalm 34

- Refuse to settle in the rut. (Psalm 40; Luke 17:11–19; Matthew 15:22) Bartimaeus wouldn't settle for blindness. He wouldn't stop until he recovered his sight. (Mark 10:52)

- Realize that God WANTS you to come to Him and to ask Him to HELP you. (Isaiah 41:10-13; 40:1-3)

- He has promised you restoration and recovery. And all the promises of God are YES. (2 Corinthians 1:20; Numbers 23:19)

- Believe the promise: The thief has to repay sevenfold what he's stolen. (Proverbs 6:31; John 10:10) The devil is the thief. And Jesus has defeated him. He has given us authority over him. You have the right to get your stuff back. Jesus paid for it. Whatever good thing that has been lost in your life, is coming back

• Prophesy to the dry bones in your life. Speak to whatever is lost and command it to come back. (Ezekiel 37:4) Use your words. Job 22:28 says, "I shall decree a thing and it will be so."

• Pray with expectation (Proverbs 23:18; Ephesians 3:20) Expect FRESH START! "You shall surely overtake your enemies and you shall recover all" (1 Samuel 30:8).

I declare that in the journey of fast-tracking my Fresh Start with prayer, I shall recover all that has been lost in my life. I expect the restoration of lost relationships, lost money, lost hope, and lost opportunities, lost esteem, honor, potentials and possibilities. I will not settle for less of what God has for me.

AMEN! GLORY! HALLELUJAH!

ABOUT DAMOLA

Damola Treasure Okenla (DTO) is the author of several Christian and inspirational books, a sought-after inspirational speaker, certified life coach, and transformational prayer strategist. She has dedicated her life to uplifting others and helping her clients grow and develop spiritually.

DTO is also the president and founder of Life Encounters Incorporated, a not-for-profit organization dedicated to self-discovery and recovery through seminars, workshops, and retreats. Her organization, like her books, reflects her passion and mission to advocate spiritual freedom and empowerment of individuals.

Her website is www.damolatreasureokenla.com

FOLLOW DAMOLA:

https://www.facebook.com/damola.okenla

https://www.instagram.com/dtoinspirations/

https://twitter.com/DTO03

FB Groups

https://www.facebook.com/groups/purposelyempoweredwoman/

https://www.facebook.com/groups/transformationalprayersnetwork/